FREE PREMIUM BONUS!

#1. Download **CHAKRA-INDEX IN COLOR**. *SCAN QR-CODE or go to:*

https://rb.gy/iof2om

VIVEKACHUDAMANI
CREST-JEWEL OF
DISCRIMINATION

Graphic Design
Mattias Långström

VIVEKACHUDAMANI
CREST-JEWEL OF DISCRIMINATION

Translation and comments
Jan Fahleman

ISBN 9789198915327

✸✸✸

Copyright © Jan Fahleman

2024

PREFACE

Sri Adi Shankara is the author of Vivekachudamani, which can be translated as "Crest-Jewel of discrimination". By distinguishing the real from the illusion, the truth can emerge. In 580 verses, Shankara has shown man's attachment to the unreal illusion and the path to liberation. The basis of his philosophy is the non-dualistic Advaita Vedanta.

Sri Adi Shankara lived during the late 7th and early 8th centuries in India. His guru (teacher) was Govindapada. Shankara had numerous disciples who accompanied him during his wanderings in India. During these wanderings he met scribes from various spiritual sects and religions whom he was eager to meet in spiritual discussions. He established the path to attain salvation by removing all obstacles and closed to all questionable interpretations.

He has commented on many of the sacred scriptures of Hinduism such as; Brahma-sutras, Bhagavadgita and the Upanishads, but he has also written a number of his own books to illuminate Advaita Vedanta. Shankara died early, he was then 32 years old.

Shankara's non-dualistic Advaita Vedanta emerges from a presence in Ātman and appears as a timeless eternal wisdom. However, Shankara has used some words and expressions from the zeitgeist in which he lived during the late 7th and early 8th centuries in India. I have tried in my comments to use the words and comments of today without disturbing the timeless truths that exist beyond the words. My comments are written in italics.

Jan Fahleman.

1. I bow to Govinda, whose nature is Bliss
Supreme, who is the Sadguru, who can be
known only from the import of all Vedanta,
and who is beyond the reach of speech and
mind.

*Govinda is a name of God and the aspect of
God as the sustainer, Vishnu. Sadguru is the
divinity who stands above the Guru.*

2. For all beings a human birth is difficult
to obtain, more so is a male body; rarer
than that is Brahmanahood; rarer still is the
attachment to the path of Vedic religion;
higher than this is erudition in the scriptures;
discrimination between the Self and not-Self,
Realisation, and continuing in a state of identity with Brahman – these come next in order. (This kind of) Mukti (Liberation) is not
to be attained except through the well-earned
merits of a hundred crore of births.

*It is important to seize the opportunity to
reach liberation (Mukti) since the possibility of*

this exists in this life, and not to waste life on unessentials.

3. These are three things which are rare indeed and are due to the grace of God – namely; a human birth, the longing for Liberation, and the protecting care of a perfected sage.

All these conditions are necessary to obtain liberation (Mukti).

4. The man who, having by some means obtained a human birth, with a male body and mastery of the Vedas to boot, is foolish enough not to exert himself for self-liberation, verily commits suicide, for he kills himself by clinging to things unreal.

5. What greater fool is there than the man who having obtained a rare human body, and a masculine body too, neglects to achieve the real end of this life?

The real end of this life means liberation from the unreal ie. the identification with the relative mind and the desires of the mind to instead identify with the absolute eternal Ātman.

6. Let people quote the Scriptures and sacrifice to the gods, let them perform rituals and worship the deities, but there is no Liberation without the realisation of one's identity with the Atman, no, not even in the lifetime of a hundred Brahmas put together.

A day for the creative Brahma is 432 million human years.

7. There is no hope of immortality by means of riches – such indeed is the declaration of the Vedas. Hence it is clear that works cannot be the cause of Liberation.

Riches have the ability to bind the attention to the relative sensuality which draws the attention away from liberation. The mind can never be the cause of liberation.

8. Therefore the man of learning should strive his best for Liberation, having renounced his desire for pleasures from external objects, duly approaching a good and generous preceptor, and fixing his mind on the truth inculcated by him.

9. Having attained the Yogarudha state, one should recover oneself, immersed in the sea of birth and death by means of devotion to right discrimination.

The state of Yogārūtha a arises by applying Yoga through devotion and distinguishing the real from the unreal illusion.

10. Let the wise and erudite man, having commenced the practice of the realisation of the Atman give up all works and try to cut loose the bonds of birth and death.

11. Work leads to purification of the mind, not to perception of the Reality. The realisation of Truth is brought about by discrimi-

nation and not in the least by ten million of acts.

Work in the form of Yoga exercises purifies the body and mind. Discrimination facilitates the realization of the Truth.

12. By adequate reasoning the conviction of the reality about the rope is gained, which puts an end to the great fear and misery caused by the snake worked up in the deluded mind.

Shankara often brings up the anecdote of a rope in a dark room being perceived to be a snake and the fear that then arises, until the truth is revealed, ie. that the snake was a rope.

13. The conviction of the Truth is seen to proceed from reasoning upon the salutary counsel of the wise, and not by bathing in the sacred waters, nor by gifts, nor by a hundred Pranayamas (control of the vital force).

14. Success depends essentially on a qualified aspirant; time, place and other such means are but auxiliaries in this regard.

The time and space dimension has subordinate importance then that is to experience the Truth.

15. Hence the seeker after the Reality of the Atman should take to reasoning, after duly approaching the Guru – who should be the best of the knowers of Brahman, and an ocean of mercy.

Having access to someone who has knowledge of the reality of Ātman, is important, in order to gain intellectual knowledge, (Jnana-Yoga). This is important to be able to distinguish Truth from illusion by reasoning and realize that Ātman and Brahman are identical.

16. An intelligent and learned man skilled in arguing in favour of the Scriptures and in refuting counter-arguments against them

– one who has got the above characteristics is the fit recipient of the knowledge of the Atman.

The purpose of refuting counterarguments is not to win an argument but to dispel ignorance.

17. The man who discriminates between the Real and the unreal, whose mind is turned away from the unreal, who possesses calmness and the allied virtues, and who is longing for Liberation, is alone considered qualified to enquire after Brahman.

Whoever has the above spiritual maturity also has the ability to communicate with Godconsciousness.

18. Regarding this, sages have spoken of four means of attainment, which alone being present, the devotion to Brahman succeeds, and in the absence of which, it fails.

19. First is; enumerated discrimination between the Real and the unreal, next comes aversion to the enjoyment of fruits (of one's actions) here and hereafter, (next is) the group of six attributes, viz. calmness and the rest, and (last) is clearly the yearning for Liberation.

20. A firm conviction of the mind to the effect that Brahman is real and the universe unreal, is designated as discrimination (Viveka) between the Real and the unreal.

21. Vairagya or renunciation is the desire to give up all transitory enjoyments (ranging) from those of an (animate) body to those of Brahmahood (having already known their defects) from observation, instruction and so forth.

It is not the temporary pleasures that bind to the unreal that are the problem, but the desire for them. It does not help to get rid of the objects of pleasure as long as the desire for them remains. As long as desire remains, it will seek the objects of pleasure and be mentally attached to them.

22. The resting of the mind steadfastly on its Goal (viz. Brahman) after having detached itself from manifold sense-objects by continually observing their defects, is called Shama or calmness.

Having taken control of the desire for sense objects means that the constant search for more sense gratification ceases and Śama or tranquility arises.

23. Turning both kinds of sense-organs away from sense-objects and placing them in their respective centres, is called Dama or self-control. The best Uparati or self-withdrawal consists in the mind-function ceasing to be affected by external objects.

24. The bearing of all afflictions without caring to redress them, being free (at the same

time) from anxiety or lament on their score,
is called Titiksha or forbearance.

*To have patience (Titiksā), is to accept exis-
tence as it is, as it cannot be different in the
present.*

25. Acceptance by firm judgment as true of
what the Scriptures and the Guru instruct, is
called by sages Shraddha or faith, by means
of which the Reality is perceived.

*Blind faith is relying totally on external in-
formation from scriptures or from the Guru,
while credence based on an inner feeling that
arises due to the external information and is
connected with the insight that the information arouses.*

26. Not the mere indulgence of thought (in
curiosity) but the constant concentration of
the intellect (or the affirming faculty) on the
ever-pure Brahman, is what is called Samad-
hana or self-settledness.

*To be constantly present in Brahman, the
highest state of Consciousness when thought
and intellect and desires are transcended and
erased, which means the total satisfaction, bliss
(the self-satisfaction Samādhāna).*

27. Mumukshuta or yearning for Freedom is
the desire to free oneself, by realising one's
true nature, from all bondages from that of
egoism to that of the body – bondages superimposed by Ignorance.

*Freedom – Mumuksutā, can only arise when
ignorance is replaced by knowledge of the true
reality.*

28. Even though torpid or mediocre, this
yearning for Freedom, through the grace of
the Guru, may bear fruit (being developed)
by means of Vairagya (renunciation), Shama
(calmness), and so on.

*The Guru's grace gives extra energy and spiri-
tual presence that gives better opportunities to
control desires and establish peace.*

29. In his case, verily, whose renunciation
and yearning for Freedom are intense, calmness and the other practices have (really)
their meaning and bear fruit.

30. Where (however) this renunciation
and yearning for Freedom are torpid, there
calmness and the other practices are as mere
appearances, like water in a desert.

31. Among things conducive to Liberation,
devotion (Bhakti) holds the supreme place.
The seeking after one's real nature is designated as devotion.

*To search devotedly for one's true nature re-
gardless of adversity and difficulty and not to
give up, is Bhakti.*

32. Others maintain that the inquiry into
the truth of one's own self is devotion. The
inquirer about the truth of the Atman who is
possessed of the above-mentioned means of
attainment should approach a wise preceptor,
who confers emancipation from bondage.

33. Who is versed in the Vedas, sinless, un-smitten by desire and a knower of Brahman par excellence, who has withdrawn himself into Brahman; who is calm, like fire that has consumed its fuel, who is a boundless reservoir of mercy that knows no reason, and a friend of all good people who prostrate themselves before him.

34. Worshipping that Guru with devotion, and approaching him, when he is pleased with prostration, humility and service, (he) should ask him what he has got to know:

35. O Master, O friend of those that bow to thee, thou ocean of mercy, I bow to thee; save me, fallen as I am into this sea of birth and death, with a straightforward glance of thine eye, which sheds nectar-like grace supreme.

36. Save me from death, afflicted as I am by the unquenchable fire of this world-forest, and shaken violently by the winds of an untoward lot, terrified and (so) seeking refuge in thee, for I do not know of any other man with whom to seek shelter.

37. There are good souls, calm and magnanimous, who do good to others as does the spring, and who, having themselves crossed this dreadful ocean of birth and death, help others also to cross the same, without any motive whatsoever.

There are good souls who help others without any ulterior motives to receive something in return.

38. It is the very nature of the magnanimous to move of their own accord towards removing others' troubles. Here, for instance, is the moon who, as everybody knows, voluntarily saves the earth parched by the flaming rays of the sun.

39. O Lord, with thy nectar-like speech, sweetened by the enjoyment of the elixir – like bliss of Brahman, pure, cooling to a degree, issuing in streams from thy lips as from a pitcher, and delightful to the ear – do thou sprinkle me who am tormented by worldly afflictions as by the tongues of a forest-fire. Blessed are those on whom even a passing glance of thy eye lights, accepting them as thine own.

40. How to cross this ocean of phenomenal existence, what is to be my fate, and which of the means should I adopt – as to these I know nothing. Condescend to save me, O Lord, and describe at length how to put an end to the misery of this relative existence.

The seeker has come to the conclusion that relative existence causes suffering and wants help in ending the misery. This is the starting point for a cry for help.

41. As he speaks thus, tormented by the

afflictions of the world – which is like a forest
on fire - and seeking his protection, the saint
eyes him with a glance softened with pity and
spontaneously bids him give up all fear.

*In this state of awareness that the seeker is in,
the saint sees him as ripe to share his knowledge.*

42. To him who has sought his protection,
thirsting for Liberation, who duly obeys
the injunctions of the Scriptures, who is of a
serene mind, and endowed with calmness -
(to such a one) the sage proceeds to inculcate
the truth out of sheer grace.

43. Fear not, O learned one, there is no death
for thee; there is a means of crossing this sea
of relative existence; that very way by which
sages have gone beyond it, I shall inculcate to
thee.

*The path that the sages have gone beyond
refers to the knowledge that is beyond the
intellectual knowledge of the mind.*

44. There is a sovereign means which puts an end to the fear of relative existence; through that thou wilt cross the sea of Samsara and attain the supreme bliss.

45. Reasoning on the meaning of the Vedanta leads to efficient knowledge, which is immediately followed by the total annihilation of the misery born of relative existence.

46. Faith (Shraddha), devotion and the Yoga of meditation – these are mentioned by the Shruti as the immediate factors of Liberation in the case of a seeker; whoever abides in these gets Liberation from the bondage of the body, which is the conjuring of Ignorance.

Being focused, dedicated and present in Yoga as well as having faith in spiritual development are cornerstones when it comes to being freed from the illusions of ignorance.

47. It is verily through the touch of Ignorance that thou who art the Supreme Self findest

thyself under the bondage of the non-Self,
whence alone proceeds the round of births
and deaths. The fire of knowledge, kindled by
the discrimination between these two, burns
up the effects of Ignorance together with
their root.

*It is only by gaining insight and knowledge
of the non-self (mind) and the Self (Consciousness) that the school of life has fulfilled its
purpose and ignorance is annihilated.*

48. Condescend to listen, O Master, to the
question I am putting (to thee). I shall be
gratified to hear a reply to the same from thy
lips.

49. What is bondage, forsooth? How has it
come (upon the Self)? How does it continue
to exist ? How is one freed from it? What
is this non-Self? And who is the Supreme
Self? And how can one discriminate between
them? Do tell me about all these.

50. The Guru replied: Blessed art thou ! Thou hast achieved thy life's end and hast sanctified thy family, that thou wishest to attain Brahmanhood by getting free from the bondage of Ignorance !

51. A father has got his sons and others to free him from his debts, but he has got none but himself to remove his bondage.

One can get comfort and advice from others, but to become aware and gain spiritual insights, the awareness must come from within.

52. Trouble such as that caused by a load on the head can be removed by others, but none but one's own self can put a stop to the pain which is caused by hunger and the like.

53. The patient who takes (the proper) diet

and medicine is alone seen to recover completely – not through work done by others.

54. The true nature of things is to be known personally, through the eye of clear illumination, and not through a sage: what the moon exactly is, is to be known with one's own eyes; can others make him know it?

55. Who but one's own self can get rid of the bondage caused by the fetters of Ignorance, desire, action and the like, aye even in a hundred crore of cycles?

Cycles mean ages, a kalpa contains 4.32 billion years.

56. Neither by Yoga, nor by Sankhya, nor by work, nor by learning, but by the realisation of one's identity with Brahman is Liberation possible, and by no other means.

57. The beauty of a guitar's form and the skill of playing on its chords serve merely to plea-

se a few persons; they do not suffice to confer
sovereignty.

*Playing the guitar can stimulate creativity but
is not enough to reach spiritual realization.*

58. Loud speech consisting of a shower of
words, the skill in expounding the Scriptures,
and likewise erudition – these merely bring
on a little personal enjoyment to the scholar,
but are no good for Liberation.

*To be freed from the illusion contributed by the
mind and intellect cannot be resolved intel-
lectually. Liberation must take place through
presence in Consciousness.*

59. The study of the Scriptures is useless so
long as the highest Truth is unknown, and it
is equally useless when the highest Truth has
already been known.

*Before the Truth is experienced, the Scriptures
cannot be understood and they serve no func-*

*tion when the Truth is understood, other than
as a confirmation.*

60. The Scriptures consisting of many words
are a dense forest which merely causes the
mind to ramble. Hence men of wisdom
should earnestly set about knowing the true
nature of the Self.

*Scriptures can cause the mind and intellect
to become enslaved by musings and thought
constructs instead of being present in the pure
nature of Consciousness.*

61. For one who has been bitten by the
serpent of Ignorance, the only remedy is the
knowledge of Brahman. Of what avail are the
Vedas and (other) Scriptures, Mantras (sacred formulae) and medicines to such a one?

*Vedas and other scriptures, mantras and medi-
cines can be aids, but never become the cause
of permanent conscious presence in Consciousness. It is always divine grace that is the cause.*

62. A disease does not leave off if one simply utter the name of the medicine, without taking it; (similarly) without direct realisation one cannot be liberated by the mere utterance of the word Brahman.

Just believing in spirituality and believing in Consciousness does not help to be freed from ignorance.

63. Without causing the objective universe to vanish and without knowing the truth of the Self, how is one to achieve Liberation by the mere utterance of the word Brahman? It would result merely in an effort of speech.

By believing only in absolute existence, relative existence does not disappear.

64. Without killing one's enemies, and possessing oneself of the splendour of the entire surrounding region, one cannot claim to be an emperor by merely saying, 'I am an emperor'.

65. As a treasure hidden underground requires (for its extraction) competent instruction, excavation, the removal of stones and other such things lying above it and (finally) grasping, but never comes out by being (merely) called out by name, so the transparent Truth of the self, which is hidden by Maya and its effects, is to be attained through the instructions of a knower of Brahman, followed by reflection, meditation and so forth, but not through perverted arguments.

Only by being consciously present in Consciousness can the truth of Consciousness become reality. It is this knowledge that gives insight and liberation from ignorance.

66. Therefore the wise should, as in the case of disease and the like, personally strive by all the means in their power to be free from the bondage of repeated births and deaths.

67. The question that thou hast asked today is excellent, approved by those versed in the

Scriptures, aphoristic, pregnant with meaning and fit to be known by the seekers after Liberation.

Asking questions is often the gateway to knowledge.

68. Listen attentively, O learned one, to what I am going to say. By listening to it thou shalt be instantly free from the bondage of Samsara.

69. The first step to Liberation is the extreme aversion to all perishable things, then follow calmness, self-control, forbearance, and the utter relinquishment of all work enjoined in the Scriptures.

70. Then come hearing, reflection on that, and long, constant and unbroken meditation on the Truth for the Muni. After that the learned seeker attains the supreme Nirvikalpa state and realises the bliss of Nirvana even in this life.

After practicing meditation, Nirvikalpa Samadhi can be maintained, which is presence in Consciousness.

71. Now I am going to tell thee fully about what thou oughtst to know – the discrimination between the Self and the non-Self. Listen to it and decide about it in thy mind.

72. Composed of the seven ingredients, viz. marrow, bones, fat, flesh, blood, skin and cuticle, and consisting of the following limbs and their parts – legs, thighs, the chest, arms, the back and the head:

73. This body, reputed to be the abode of the delusion of 'I and mine', is designated by sages as the gross body. The sky, air, fire, water and earth are subtle elements.

74. Being united with parts of one another and becoming gross, (they) form the gross body. And their subtle essences form sense-objects - the group of five such as sound,

which conduce to the happiness of the experiencer, the individual soul.

75. Those fools who are tied to these sense-objects by the stout cord of attachment, so very difficult to snap, come and depart, up and down, carried amain by the powerful emissary of their past action.

The mind is not something to be defeated or annihilated. The mind loses its attractiveness when presence in Consciousness arises, unnecessary mind activity disappears as presence in Consciousness becomes stronger. The experience then arises that; I am not the body, I have a body that I witness. The body is then seen as a tool.

76. The deer, the elephant, the moth, the fish and the black-bee – these five have died, being tied to one or other of the five senses, viz. sound etc., through their own attachment. What then is in store for man who is attached to all these five.

77. Sense-objects are even more virulent in their evil effects than the poison of the cobra. Poison kills one who takes it, but those others kill one who even looks at them through the eyes.

78. He who is free from the terrible snare of the hankering after sense-objects, so very difficult to get rid of, is alone fit for Liberation, and none else – even though he be versed in all the six Shastras.

As the mind no longer dominates awareness, the desire for sense pleasure can also be gone. Independent, even if one is versed in the Śastras, which are sacred scriptures.

79. The shark of hankering catches by the throat those seekers after Liberation who have got only an apparent dispassion (Vairagya) and are trying to cross the ocean of samsara (relative existence), and violently snatching them away, drowns them half-way.

80. He who has killed the shark known as sense-object with the sword of mature dispassion, crosses the ocean of Samsara, free from all obstacles.

81. Know that death quickly overtakes the stupid man who walks along the dreadful ways of sense-pleasure; whereas one who walks in accordance with the instructions of a well-wishing and worthy Guru, as also with his own reasoning, achieves his end - know this to be true.

82. If indeed thou hast a craving for Liberation, shun sense-objects from a good distance as thou wouldst do poison, and always

cultivate carefully the nectar-like virtues
of contentment, compassion, forgiveness,
straight-forwardness, calmness and self-control.

83. Whoever leaves aside what should always
be attempted, viz. emancipation from the
bondage of Ignorance without beginning,
and passionately seeks to nourish this body,
which is an object for others to enjoy, commits suicide thereby.

*Those who are body-fixated have difficulty
freeing themselves from their body and mind.
They must begin to investigate what this fixa-
tion leads to.*

84. Whoever seeks to realise the Self by devoting himself to the nourishment of the body,
proceeds to cross a river by catching hold of a
crocodile, mistaking it for a log.

85. So for a seeker after Liberation the infatuation over things like the body is a dire death.

He who has thoroughly conquered this deserves the state of Freedom.

86. Conquer the dire death of infatuation over thy body, wife, children etc. conquering which the sages reach that Supreme State of Vishnu.

87. This gross body is to be deprecated, for it consists of the skin, flesh, blood, arteries and veins, fat, marrow and bones, and is full of other offensive things.

For some, seeing the body as something repulsive can temporarily reduce the desire for the bodily.

88. The gross body is produced by one's past actions out of the gross elements formed by the union of the subtle elements with each other, and is the medium of experience for the soul. That is its waking state in which it perceives gross objects.

89. Identifying itself with this form, the individual soul, though separate, enjoys gross objects, such as garlands and sandal-paste, by means of the external organs. Hence this body has its fullest play in the waking state.

90. Know this gross body to be like a house to the householder, on which rests man's entire dealing with the external world.

91. Birth, decay and death are the various characteristics of the gross body, as also stoutness etc., childhood etc., are its different conditions; it has got various restrictions regarding castes and orders of life; it is subject to various diseases, and meets with different kinds of treatment, such as worship, insult and high honours.

92. The ears, skin, eyes, nose and tongue are organs of knowledge, for they help us to cognise objects; the vocal organs, hands, legs, etc., are organs of action, owing to their tendency to work.

93-94. The inner organ (Antahkarana) is called Manas, Buddhi, ego or Chitta, according to their respective functions: Manas, from its considering the pros and cons of a thing; Buddhi, from its property of determining the truth of objects; the ego, from its identification with this body as one's own self; and Chitta, from its function of remembering things it is interested in.

Antahkarana is the internal system consisting of; Manas – mind, Buddhi – intellect, Chitta – memory, Ahamkara – ego.

95. One and the same Prana (vital force) becomes Prana, Apana, Vyana, Udana and Samana according to their diversity of functions and modifications, like gold, water, etc.

Prana means life force and consists of; Apāna, Vyāna, Udāna, Samāna, all of which administer the breath and life force in different parts of the body.

96. The five organs of action such as speech, the five organs of knowledge such as the ear, the group of five Pranas, the five elements ending with the ether, together with Buddhi and the rest as also Nescience, desire and action - these eight "cities" make up what is called the subtle body.

97. Listen - this subtle body, called also the Linga body, is produced out of the elements before their subdividing and combining with each other, is possessed of latent impressions and causes the soul to experience the fruits of its past actions.

It is a beginningless superimposition on the soul brought on by its own ignorance.

98-99. Dream is a state of the soul distinct from the waking state, where it shines by itself. In dreams Buddhi, by itself, takes on the role of the agent and the like, owing to various latent impressions of the waking state, while the supreme Atman shines in Its own glory - with Buddhi as Its only superimposition, the witness of everything, and is not touched by the least work that Buddhi does. As It is wholly unattached, It is not touched by any work that Its superimpositions may perform.

The dream is a state of consciousness created by wishes and desires that the intellect (Buddhi) stages. The Ātman which is free from all desires and cravings is not affected by this state of consciousness.

100. This subtle body is the instrument for all activities of the Atman, who is Knowledge Absolute, like the adze and other tools of a carpenter. Therefore this Atman is perfectly unattached.

101. Blindness, weakness and sharpness are conditions of the eye, due merely to its fitness or defectiveness; so are deafness, dumbness, etc., of the ear and so forth - but never of the Atman, the Knower.

102. Inhalation and exhalation, yawning, sneezing, secretion, leaving this body, etc., are called by experts functions of Prana and the rest, while hunger and thirst are characteristics of Prana proper.

Hunger and thirst sustain the life force, Prāna.

103. The inner organ (mind) has its seat in the organs such as the eye, as well as in the body, identifying with them and endued with a reflection of the Atman.

Mind identifies itself with all relative mind functions but at the same time the absolute exists – Ātman.

104. Know that it is egoism which, identifying itself with the body, becomes the doer or experiencer, and in conjunction with the Gunas such as the Sattva, assumes the three different states.

Gunas are, tamas, rajas and sattva that exist

in the states of consciousness sleep, dream and wakefulness.

105. When sense-objects are favourable it becomes happy, and it becomes miserable when the case is contrary. So happiness and misery are characteristics of egoism, and not of the ever-blissful Atman.

The ego creates temporary moods that result in happiness, or duality and conflict, while the Ātman is unaffected.

106. Sense-objects are pleasurable only as dependent on the Atman manifesting through them, and not independently, because the Atman is by Its very nature the most beloved of all. Therefore the Atman is ever blissful, and never suffers misery.

He who is consciously present in Ātman does not suffer, but is always free.

107. That in profound sleep we experience

the bliss of the Atman independent of sense-objects, is clearly attested by the Shruti, direct perception, tradition and inference.

108. Avidya (Nescience) or Maya, called also the Undifferentiated, is the power of the Lord. She is without beginning, is made up of the three Gunas and is superior to the effects (as their cause). She is to be inferred by one of clear intellect only from the effects She produces. It is She who brings forth this whole universe.

Māyā or relative existence is eternally ongoing force which, however, depends on dominating the present awareness in the present moment. Through presence in Consciousness, the effects produced by ignorance are reduced.

109. She is neither existent nor non-existent nor partaking of both characters; neither same nor different nor both; neither composed of parts nor an indivisible whole nor both. She is most wonderful and cannot be described in words.

110. Maya can be destroyed by the realisation of the pure Brahman, the one without a second, just as the mistaken idea of a snake is removed by the discrimination of the rope. She has her Gunas as Rajas, Tamas and Sattva, named after their respective functions.

111. Rajas has its Vikshepa-Shakti or projecting power, which is of the nature of an activity, and from which this primeval flow of activity has emanated. From this also, mental modifications such as attachment and grief are continually produced.

*Rajas is characterized by activity that often
leads to mental attachments and sorrow.*

112. Lust, anger, avarice, arrogance, spite, egoism, envy, jealousy, etc., these are the dire attributes of Rajas, from which the worldly

tendency of man is produced. Therefore Rajas is a cause of bondage.

The qualities that are the cause of Rajas can also be seen as the mind with its limiting and narrow-minded awareness.

113. Avriti or the veiling power is the power of Tamas, which makes things appear other than what they are. It is this that causes man's repeated transmigrations, and starts the action of the projecting power (Vikshepa).

Tamas causes ignorance and confusion. It is tamas that causes destructive energies to work in existence.

114. Even wise and learned men and men who are clever and adept in the vision of the exceedingly subtle Atman, are overpowered by Tamas and do not understand the Atman, even though clearly explained in various ways. What is simply superimposed by delusion, they consider as true, and attach them-

selves to its effects. Alas! How powerful is the great Avriti Shakti of dreadful Tamas!

115. Absence of the right judgment, or contrary judgment, want of definite belief and doubt - these certainly never desert one who has any connection with this veiling power, and then the projecting power gives ceaseless trouble.

116. Ignorance, lassitude, dullness, sleep, inadvertence, stupidity, etc., are attributes of Tamas. One tied to these does not comprehend anything, but remains like one asleep or like a stock or stone.

Tamas which veils the true and real is always noticed by pure Consciousness.

117. Pure Sattva is (clear) like water, yet in conjunction with Rajas and Tamas it makes for transmigration. The reality of the Atman becomes reflected in Sattva and like the sun reveals the entire world of matter.

Both Sattva, Rajas and Tamas are relative qualities which do not belong to the absolute status of Ātman which remains untouched. and therefore they belong to Māyā and thus are subject to rebirth.

118. The traits of mixed Sattva are an utter absence of pride etc., and Niyama, Yama, etc., as well as faith, devotion, yearning for Liberation, the divine tendencies and turning away from the unreal.

Niyama are rules of life and Yama are qualities; with the aim of providing purity and harmony. Sattva provides the conditions for developing spiritual qualities.

119. The traits of pure Sattva are cheerfulness, the realisation of one's own Self, supreme peace, contentment, bliss, and steady devotion to the Atman, by which the aspirant enjoys bliss everlasting.

Pure Sattva can exist when only Sattva prevails unhindered.

120. This Undifferentiated, spoken of as the compound of the three Gunas, is the causal body of the soul. Profound sleep is its special state, in which the functions of the mind and all its organs are suspended.

The causal body is the mental body of the mind in which the three Gunas operate. Deep sleep is the state of mind in which consciousness is dormant. Ātman, however, is always present, even during deep sleep.

121. Profound sleep is the cessation of all kinds of perception, in which the mind remains in a subtle seed-like form. The test of

this is the universal verdict, "I did not know anything then".

During deep sleep, the intellect and emotions are completely disconnected. No conceptual memory can then emerge.

122. The body, organs, Pranas, Manas, egoism, etc., all modifications, the sense-objects, pleasure and the rest, the gross elements such as the ether, in fact, the whole universe, up to the Undifferentiated - all this is the non-Self.

The relative mind that is often confused with the Self, can be seen as tools used to navigate conceptual existence.

123. From Mahat down to the gross body everything is the effect of Maya: These and Maya itself know thou to be the non-Self, and therefore unreal like the mirage in a desert.

Mahat is the intelligence of relative existence

*which encompasses and is the effect of Māyā. It
is aware that the non-self is the unreal self.*

124. Now I am going to tell thee of the real
nature of the supreme Self, realising which
man is freed from bondage and attains Liberation.

125. There is some Absolute Entity, the
eternal substratum of the consciousness of
egoism, the witness of the three states, and
distinct from the five sheaths or coverings:

*The five sheaths are; Anna matter, Prana life
force, Mana mind, Vijnana knowledge and
Ananda bliss.*

126. Which knows everything that happens
in the waking state, in dream and in profound sleep; which is aware of the presence
or absence of the mind and its functions;
and which is the background of the notion of
egoism. This is That.

127. Which Itself sees all, but which no one
beholds, which illumines the intellect etc.,
but which they cannot illumine. - This is
That.

*Consciousness is not an object that can be
observed.*

128. By which this universe is pervaded, but
which nothing pervades, which shining, all
this (universe) shines as Its reflection. - This
is That.

129. By whose very presence the body, the organs, mind and intellect keep to their respective spheres of action, like servants!

*The various functions of the mind serve as
tools in relative existence.*

130. By which everything from egoism down
to the body, the sense-objects and pleasure
etc., is known as palpably as a jar - for It is
the essence of Eternal Knowledge!

In the same way that the material tools serve, so do the immaterial tools such as egoism and the desires of the mind.

131. This is the innermost Self, the primeval Purusha (Being), whose essence is the constant realisation of infinite Bliss, which is ever the same, yet reflecting through the different mental modifications, and commanded by which the organs and Pranas perform their functions.

It is Purusha (Consciousness) that encompasses and is the hub of both absolute and relative existence.

132. In this very body, in the mind full of Sattva, in the secret chamber of the intellect, in the Akasha known as the Unmanifested, the Atman, of charming splendour, shines like the sun aloft, manifesting this universe through Its own effulgence.

133. The Knower of the modifications of

mind and egoism, and of the activities of the
body, the organs and Pranas, apparently taking their forms, like the fire in a ball of iron;
It neither acts nor is subject to change in the
least.

134. It is neither born nor dies, It neither
grows nor decays, nor does It undergo any
change, being eternal. It does not cease to
exist even when this body is destroyed, like
the sky in a jar (after it is broken), for It is
independent.

*Ātman's existence is not dependent on any-
thing.*

135. The Supreme Self, different from the
Prakriti and its modifications, of the essence
of Pure Knowledge, and Absolute, directly
manifests this entire gross and subtle universe, in the waking and other states, as the substratum of the persistent sense of egoism, and
manifests Itself as the Witness of the Buddhi,
the determinative faculty.

Paramātmā, the pure Consciousness, is all-pervading and without modification, while the mind, ego and intellect change accoding to the prevailing state of consciousness.

136. By means of a regulated mind and the purified intellect (Buddhi), realise directly thy own Self in the body so as to identify thyself with It, cross the boundless ocean of Samsara whose waves are birth and death, and firmly established in Brahman as thy own essence, be blessed.

137. Identifying the Self with this non-Self - this is the bondage of man, which is due to his ignorance, and brings in its train the miseries of birth and death. It is through this that one considers this evanescent body as real, and identifying oneself with it, nouris- hes, bathes, and preserves it by means of (ag- reeable) sense-objects, by which he becomes bound as the caterpillar by the threads of its cocoon.

*Being constantly present in sense sensations
means an attachment to the mind that leads
to an identification with the mind. Only by
simultaneously being present in Consciousness
can discrimination arise and ignorance be
removed.*

138. One who is overpowered by ignorance mistakes a thing for what it is not; It is the absence of discrimination that causes one to mistake a snake for a rope, and great dangers overtake him when he seizes it through that wrong notion. Hence, listen, my friend, it is the mistaking of transitory things as real that constitutes bondage.

139. This veiling power (Avriti), which preponderates in ignorance, covers the Self, whose glories are infinite and which manifests Itself through the power of knowledge, indivisible, eternal and one without a second - as Rahu does the orb of the sun.

In Hindu astrology, Rahu represents mate-

*rialism, fear, dissatisfaction, obsession and
confusion.*

140. When his own Self, endowed with the
purest splendour, is hidden from view, a man
through ignorance falsely identifies himself
with this body, which is the non-Self. And
then the great power of rajas called the projecting power sorely afflicts him through the
binding fetters of lust, anger, etc.

*When ignorance through the power of rajas
can affect lust, anger, etc. arise, and when the
force of tamas affects, aggression, hatred and
revenge can arise, which are often connected
and cause suffering.*

141. The man of perverted intellect, having
his Self-knowledge swallowed up by the
shark of utter ignorance, himself imitates the
various states of the intellect (Buddhi), as that
is Its superimposed attribute, and drifts up
and down in this boundless ocean of Samsara
which is full of the poison of sense-enjoy-

ment, now sinking, now rising - a miserable fate indeed!

The result of acting in ignorance is that pure Consciousness is overshadowed.

142. As layers of clouds generated by the sun's rays cover the sun and alone appear (in the sky), so egoism generated by the Self, covers the reality of the Self and appears by itself.

Even egoism overshadows pure Consciousness.

143. Just as, on a cloudy day, when the sun is swallowed up by dense clouds, violent cold blasts trouble them, so when the Atman is hidden by intense ignorance, the dreadful Vikshepa Shakti (projecting power) afflicts the foolish man with numerous griefs.

144. It is from these two powers that man's bondage has proceeded - beguiled by which he mistakes the body for the Self and wanders (from body to body).

It is the veiling and projecting power, Viksepa Shakti, that creates attachment.

145. Of the tree of Samsara ignorance is the seed, the identification with the body is its sprout, attachment its tender leaves, work its water, the body its trunk, the vital forces its branches, the organs its twigs, the sense-objects its flowers, various miseries due to diverse works are its fruits, and the individual soul is the bird on it.

146. This bondage of the non-Self springs from ignorance, is self-caused, and is described as without beginning and end. It subjects one to the long train of miseries such as birth, death, disease and decrepitude.

The basis of ignorance is that the insight of presence in Consciousness is missing. In doing so, the mind can create a surrogate identity that enables birth, death, illness and decay.

147. This bondage can be destroyed neither

by weapons nor by wind, nor by fire, nor
by millions of acts - by nothing except the
wonderful sword of knowledge that comes of
discrimination, sharpened by the grace of the
Lord.

*Discriminating and the grace of the Lord lead
to presence in Consciousness.*

148. One who is passionately devoted to the
authority of the Shrutis acquires steadiness
in his Svadharma, which alone conduces to
the purity of his mind. The man of pure mind
realises the Supreme Self, and by this alone
Samsara with its root is destroyed.

*Sacred texts imparting knowledge of the Pa-
ramatma can help purify the mind and give
presence in Consciousness.*

149. Covered by the five sheaths - the material one and the rest - which are the products
of Its own power, the Self ceases to appear,
like the water of a tank by its accumulation of
sedge.

150. On the removal of that sedge the perfectly pure water that allays the pangs of thirst and gives immediate joy, appears unobstructed before the man.

When obstacles to presence in Consciousness are removed, joy and happiness immediately arise.

151. When all the five sheaths have been eliminated, the Self of man appears -pure, of the essence of everlasting and unalloyed bliss, indwelling, supreme and self-effulgent.

Consciousness can be totally present when the five different sheaths do not have a dominant influence on awareness.

152. To remove his bondage the wise man should discriminate between the Self and the non-Self. By that alone he comes to know his own Self as Existence-Knowledge-Bliss Absolute and becomes happy.

153. He indeed is free who discriminates
between all sense-objects and the indwelling,
unattached and inactive Self - as one separa-
tes a stalk of grass from its enveloping sheath
- and merging everything in It, remains in a
state of identity with That.

154. This body of ours is the product of food
and comprises the material sheath; it lives on
food and dies without it; it is a mass of skin,
flesh, blood, bones and filth, and can never
be the eternally pure, self-existent Atman.

155. It does not exist prior to inception or
posterior to dissolution, but lasts only for
a short (intervening) period; its virtues are
transient, and it is changeful by nature; it is
manifold, inert, and is a sense-object, like a
jar; how can it be one's own Self, the Witness
of changes in all things?

*Relative existence and absolute existence are
each other's opposites, yet are always united in
Consciousness.*

156. The body, consisting of arms, legs, etc., cannot be the Atman, for one continues to live even when particular limbs are gone, and the different functions of the organism also remain intact. The body which is subject to another's rule cannot be the Self which is the Ruler of all.

157. That the Atman as the abiding Reality is different from the body, its characteristics, its activities, its states, etc., of which It is the witness, is self-evident.

Life exists independently of the body and its properties, its activities and its states.

158. How can the body, being a pack of bones, covered with flesh, full of filth and highly impure, be the self-existent Atman, the Knower, which is ever distinct from it?

159. It is the foolish man who identifies himself with a mass of skin, flesh, fat, bones and filth, while the man of discrimination knows

his own Self, the only Reality that there is, as distinct from the body.

160. The stupid man thinks he is the body, the book-learned man identifies himself with the mixture of body and soul, while the sage possessed of realisation due to discrimination looks upon the eternal Atman as his Self, and thinks, "I am Brahman".

He who relies only on his senses believes it to be the body, while he who relies on external information may perceive it to be a mixture of body and soul, while he who is consciously present in Consciousness is Consciousness.

161. O foolish person, cease to identify thyself with this bundle of skin, flesh, fat, bones and filth, and identify thyself instead with the Absolute Brahman, the Self of all, and thus attain to supreme Peace.

162. As long as the book-learned man does not give up his mistaken identification with

the body, organs, etc., which are unreal, there
is no talk of emancipation for him, even if he
be ever so erudite in the Vedanta philosophy.

*Freeing oneself means that; was not bound by
body and mind nor by any philosophy.*

163. Just as thou dost not identify thyself
with the shadow-body, the image-body, the
dream-body, or the body thou hast in the
imaginations of thy heart, cease thou to do
likewise with the living body also.

*The shadow-body is the shadow from the body,
the image body is the image that the body makes in e.g. a mirror, the dream body is created
in the dream and the living body is the physical body.*

164. Identifications with the body alone is
the root that produces the misery of birth
etc., of people who are attached to the unreal;
therefore destroy thou this with the utmost
care. When this identification caused by the
mind is given up, there is no more chance for

rebirth.

When the mind no longer identifies with the body, life enters a new phase where rebirth no longer fulfills any function.

165. The Prana, with which we are all familiar, coupled with the five organs of action, forms the vital sheath, permeated by which the material sheath engages itself in all activities as if it were living.

In order for the body to be alive and active, Prāna, the life force, is required.

166. Neither is the vital sheath the Self - because it is a modification of Vayu, and like the air it enters into and comes out of the body, and because it never knows in the least either its own weal and woe or those of others, being eternally dependent on the Self.

167. The organs of knowledge together with the mind form the mental sheath - the cause of the diversity of things such as "I" and

"mine". It is powerful and endued with the faculty of creating differences of name etc., It manifests itself as permeating the preceding, i.e. the vital sheath.

It is from the mental shell that the ego emerges and wants to assert itself.

The organs of knowledge are the intellect and memory, which constitute the mind, which operates with a mental presence that creates "I" and "mine." Thereby, "name differences" can be created, i.e. various kinds of relative differences are experienced, which make both "my" mind and the objects unique.

168. The mental sheath is the (sacrificial) fire which, fed with the fuel of numerous desires by the five sense-organs which serve as priests, and set ablaze by the sense-objects which act as the stream of oblations, brings about this phenomenal universe.

Sri Shankara sees the perceptible universe as a

sacrificial ritual kept going by the desires of the mind and sense organs and making the sense objects sacrificial.

169. There is no Ignorance (Avidya) outside the mind. The mind alone is Avidya, the cause of the bondage of transmigration. When that is destroyed, all else is destroyed, and when it is manifested, everything else is manifested.

It is the mind that creates ignorance because its limiting awareness. In order for ignorance to be destroyed, it is required that awareness becomes aware in Consciousness, and thus also rebirth becomes unnecessary.

170. In dreams, when there is no actual contact with the external world, the mind alone creates the whole universe consisting of the experiencer etc. Similarly in the waking state also; there is no difference. Therefore all this (phenomenal universe) is the projection of the mind.

It is the mind that creates the phenomenal relative universe regardless of the prevailing state of consciousness.

171. In dreamless sleep, when the mind is reduced to its causal state, there exists nothing (for the person asleep), as is evident from universal experience. Hence man's relative existence is simply the creation of his mind, and has no objective reality.

Dreamless sleep is a state of consciousness devoid of conscious relative experience, yet it is a relative state of consciousness that belongs to the mind and is not pure Consciousness. Based on the relative mind, an objective reality is not created but the relative existence.

172. Clouds are brought in by the wind and again driven away by the same agency. Similarly, man's bondage is caused by the mind, and Liberation too is caused by that alone.

It is said that by removing the dark clouds in

*the sky, the clear sky can reveal the sun, just as
by removing stress, attachments, desires and
impurities in the mind, pure awareness can be
present.*

173. It (first) creates an attachment in man
for the body and all other sense-objects, and
binds him through that attachment like a
beast by means of ropes.

Afterwards, the selfsame mind creates in the
individual an utter distaste for these sense-objects as if they were poison, and frees
him from the bondage.

*The individual's experiences of being bound
to the body and sense sensations can produce
distaste that can ultimately lead to liberation
from these bonds.*

174. Therefore the mind is the only cause that
brings about man's bondage or Liberation:
when tainted by the effects of Rajas it leads
to bondage, and when pure and divested of

the Rajas and Tamas elements it conduces to
Liberation.

*Tamas, Rajas and Satva are different qualities
that the mind has at different times and are
therefore relative states that the mind possesses. As long as any of these conditions prevail,
awareness is bound to them and only when
they do not affect awareness can liberation
take place and pure Consciousness can be
present.*

175. Attaining purity through a preponde-
rance of discrimination and renunciation, the
mind makes for Liberation. Hence the wise
seeker after Liberation must first strengthen
these two.

Being present in discrimination and renunciation means helping to refrain from that
which binds awareness to things that do not
lead to pure Consciousness.

When Shankara gave this scripture the title

*Vivekachudamani "The Crown Jewel of Discri-
mination" it was to emphasize the importance
of being able to differentiate. A crown jewel is
the prime and most noble jewel.*

176. In the forest-tract of sense-pleasures
there prowls a huge tiger called the mind. Let
good people who have a longing for Liberation never go there!

177. The mind continually produces for the
experiencer all sense-objects without excep-
tion, whether perceived as gross or fine, the
differences of body, caste, order of life, and
tribe, as well as the varieties of qualification,
action, means and results.

178. Deluding the Jiva, which is unattached
Pure Intelligence, and binding it by the ties
of body, organs and Pranas, the mind causes
it to wander, with ideas of "I" and "mine",
amidst the varied enjoyment of results
achieved by itself.

179. Man's transmigration is due to the evil of superimposition, and the bondage of superimposition is created by the mind alone. It is this that causes the misery of birth etc., for the man of non-discrimination who is tainted by Rajas and Tamas.

What is meant here is not distinguishing between different relative sense objects or sense sensations but distinguishing the real from the unreal.

180. Hence sages who have fathomed its secret have designated the mind as Avidya or ignorance, by which alone the universe is moved to and fro, like masses of clouds by the wind.

Avidya or ignorance are temporary views perceived by the mind which are relative ie. they change with time and environment.

181. Therefore the seeker after Liberation must carefully purify the mind. When this is

purified, Liberation is as easy of access as a
fruit on the palm of one's hand.

182. He who by means of one-pointed devotion to Liberation roots out the
attachment to sense-objects, renounces all
actions, and with faith in the Real
Brahman regularly practices hearing, etc.,
succeeds in purging the Rajasika
nature of the intellect.
To regularly practice the hearing, etc., means
that the mind through hearing and
other appropriate senses is purified by being
present in Consciousness.

183. Neither can the mental sheath be the
Supreme Self, because it has a
beginning and an end, is subject to modifications, is characterised by pain and
suffering and is an object; whereas the subject
can never be identified with the
objects of knowledge.

184. The Buddhi with its modifications and

the organs of knowledge, forms the Vijnanamaya Kosha or knowledge sheath, of the
agent, having the characteristics which is the
cause of man's transmigration.

*Buddhi ie. the intellectual faculty and memory
are the cause of man's rebirth.*

185. This knowledge sheath, which seems to
be followed by a reflection of the power of
the Chit, is a modification of the Prakriti, is
endowed with the function of knowledge,
and always wholly identifies itself with the
body, organs, etc.

*Knowledge is always tied to Consciousness
(Chit) regardless of whether the conscious presence is tied to the mind or Consciousness.*

186-187. It is without beginning, characterised by egoism, is called the Jiva, and carries
on all the activities on the relative plane.
Through previous desires it performs good
and evil actions and experiences their re-

sults. Being born in various bodies, it comes and goes, up and down. It is this knowledge sheath that has the waking, dream and other states, and experiences joy and grief.

The sensual desires give rise to many different states of consciousness such as joy, sadness, anger and sexual sensuality. As long as there is desire, there will automatically be rebirth in a body.

188. It always mistakes the duties, functions and attributes of the orders of life which belong to the body, as its own. The knowledge sheath is exceedingly effulgent, owing to its close proximity to the Supreme Self, which identifying Itself with it suffers transmigration through delusion. It is therefore a superimposition on the Self.

Ātman has no attributes or necessities of life and can never be included in, or confused with, the relative corporeal and sensuous existence.

189. The self-effulgent Atman, which is Pure Knowledge, shines in the midst of the Pranas, within the heart. Though immutable, It becomes the agent and experiencer owing to Its superimposition, the knowledge sheath.

It is important that the experiencer can distinguish between the body of knowledge and the Ātman. To be able to distinguish this requires conscious presence in Consciousness.

190. Though the Self of everything that exists, this Atman, Itself assuming the limitations of the Buddhi and wrongly identifying Itself with this totally unreal entity, looks upon Itself as something different - like earthen jars from the clay of which they are made.

To identify with something totally unreal is like not being aware that the pot and the clay are outwardly different but are actually one and the same.

191. Owing to Its connection with the su-

per-impositions, the Supreme Self, even thou
naturally perfect (transcending Nature) and
eternally unchanging, assumes the qualities
of the superimpositions and appears to act
just as they do - like the changeless fire assuming the modifications of the iron which it
turns red-hot.

*The immutable fire can be seen as the absolute
which is immovable but at the same time it
affects the relative iron. The relative and the
absolute are each other's opposites but at the
same time in unity and non-dualistic.*

192. The disciple questioned: Be it through
delusion or otherwise that the Supreme Self
has come to consider Itself as the Jiva, this superimposition is without beginning, and that
which has no beginning cannot be supposed
to have an end either.

193. Therefore the Jivahood of the soul also
must have no end, and its transmigration
must continue for ever. How then can there

be Liberation for the soul? Kindly enlighten me on this point, O revered Master.

194. The Teacher said: Thou hast rightly questioned, O learned man! Listen therefore attentively: The imagination which has been conjured up by delusion can never be accepted as a fact.

195. But for delusion there can be no connection of the Self - which is unattached, beyond activity and formless - with the objective world, as in the case of blueness etc., with reference to the sky.

The sky can be seen as Ātman, which is without attributes, while the world is relative and is experienced as having different appearances, e.g. blue color, at the same time they are connected to one existence.

196. The Jivahood of the Atman, the Witness, which is beyond qualities and beyond activity, and which is realised within as Knowledge

and Bliss Absolute - has been superimposed by the delusion of the Buddhi, and is not real. And because it is by nature an unreality, it ceases to exist when the delusion is gone.

197. It exists only so long as the delusion lasts, being caused by indiscrimination due to an illusion. The rope is supposed to be the snake only so long as the mistake lasts, and there is no more snake when the illusion has vanished. Similar is the case here.

198-199. Avidya or Nescience and its effects are likewise considered as beginningless. But with the rise of Vidya or realisation, the entire effects of Avidya, even though beginningless, are destroyed together with their root - like dreams on waking up from sleep. It is clear that the phenomenal universe, even though without beginning, is not eternal - like previous non-existence.

Through Vidyā (knowledge) the real is establis-hed and Avidya (ignorance) the unreal exis-

*tence disappears automatically, like when one
wakes up from a dream.*

200-201. Previous non-existence, even
though beginningless, is observed to have
an end. So the Jivahood which is imagined
to be in the Atman through its relation with
superimposed attributes such as the Buddhi,
is not real; whereas the other (the Atman)
is essentially different from it. The relation
between the Atman and the Buddhi is due to
a false knowledge.

202. The cessation of that superimposition
takes place through perfect knowledge, and
by no other means. Perfect knowledge, according to the Shrutis, consists in the realisation
of the identity of the individual soul and
Brahman.

*When conscious presence in the mind is
transformed into awareness in Consciousness
(Brahman) perfect knowledge prevails.*

203. This realisation is attained by a perfect discrimination between the Self andthe non-Self. Therefore one must strive for the discrimination between the individual soul and the eternal Self.

204. Just as the water which is very muddy again appears as transparent water when the mud is removed, so the Atman also manifests Its undimmed lustre when the taint has been removed.

The sutra is a description of an precence that is purified and can then be awareness in Consciousness.

205. When the unreal ceases to exist, this very individual soul is definitely realised as the eternal Self. Therefore one must make it a point completely to remove things like egoism from the eternal Self.

Egoism belonging to the unreal, binds the awareness to the mind (Jivan).

206. This knowledge sheath (Vijnanamaya Kosha) that we have been speaking of, cannot be the Supreme Self for the following reasons - because it is subject to change, is insentient, is a limited thing, an object of the senses, and is not constantly present: An unreal thing cannot indeed be taken for the real Atman.

207. The blissful sheath (Anandamaya Kosha) is that modification of Nescience which manifests itself catching a reflection of the Atman which is Bliss Absolute; whose attributes are pleasure and the rest; and which appears in view when some object agreeable to oneself presents itself. It makes itself spontaneously felt by the fortunate during the fruition of their virtuous deeds; from which every corporeal being derives great joy without the least effort.

208. The blissful sheath has its fullest play during profound sleep, while in the dreaming and wakeful states it has only a partial manifestation, occasioned by the sight of agreeable objects and so forth.

The blissful sheath can affect during deep sleep as the ability to distinguish and take a stand on experiences is not present as one has in a state of awareness where one is consciously present.

209. Nor is the blissful sheath the Supreme Self, because it is endowed with the changeful attributes, is a modification of the Prakriti, is the effect of past good deeds, and imbedded in the other sheaths which are modifications.

All physical and mental bodies are changeable and belong to Prakriti, the changeable existence.

210. When all the five sheaths have been eliminated by the reasoning on Shruti passages, what remains as the culminating point of the process, is the Witness, the Knowledge Absolute - the Atman.

211. This self-effulgent Atman which is distinct from the five sheaths, the Witness of the

three states, the Real, the Changeless, the Un-
tainted, the everlasting Bliss - is to be realised
by the wise man as his own Self.

212. The disciple questioned: After these five
sheaths have been eliminated as unreal, I
find nothing, O Master, in this universe but a
Void, the absence of everything. What entity is there left forsooth with which the wise
knower of the Self should realise his identity.

213-214. The Guru answered: Thou has
rightly said, O learned man ! Thou art clever
indeed in discrimination. That by which all
those modifications such as egoism as well as
their subsequent absence (during deep sleep)
are perceived, but which Itself is not perceived, know thou that Atman - the Knower -
through the sharpest intellect.

*It is always Ātman who witnesses the different
levels of mind. It is not the waking state of
mind that witnesses the sleep or the dream.*

215. That which is perceived by something else has for its witness the latter. When there is no agent to perceive a thing, we cannot speak of it as having been perceived at all.

216. This Atman is a self-cognised entity because It is cognised by Itself. Hence the individual soul is itself and directly the Supreme Brahman, and nothing else.

As everything is Brahman there is no dualistic relationship with Ātman or the individual mind.

217. That which clearly manifests Itself in the states of wakefulness, dream and profound sleep; which is inwardly perceived in the mind in various forms as an unbroken series of egoistic impressions; which witnesses the egoism, the Buddhi, etc., which are of diverse forms and modifications; and which makes Itself felt as the Existence-Knowledge-Bliss Absolute; know thou this Atman, thy own Self, within thy heart.

218. Seeing the reflection of the sun mirrored
in the water of a jar, the fool thinks it is the
sun itself. Similarly the stupid man, through
delusion, identifies himself with the reflection of the Chit caught in the Buddhi, which
is Its superimposition.

*Chit is Consciousness and Buddhi is the intel-
lect, which are the absolute and relative aspects
of existence respectively.*

219. Just as the wise man leaves aside the jar,
the water and the reflection of the sun in it,
and sees the self-luminous sun which illumines these three and is independent of them.

220-222. Similarly, discarding the body, the Buddhi and the reflection of the Chit in it, and realising the Witness, the Self, the Knowledge Absolute, the cause of the manifestation of everything, which is hidden in the recesses of the Buddhi, is distinct from the gross and subtle, eternal, omnipresent, all-pervading and extremely subtle, and which has neither interior nor exterior and is identical with one self - fully realising this true nature of oneself, one becomes free from sin, taint, death and grief, and becomes the embodiment of Bliss. Illumined himself, he is afraid of none. For a seeker after Liberation there is no other way to the breaking of the bonds of transmigration than the realisation of the truth of one's own Self.

The result of liberation is in the present Bliss ie. peace, freedom, tranquility and eventually liberation from rebirth.

223. The realisation of one's identity with Brahman is the cause of Liberation from

the bonds of Samsara, by means of which the wise man attains Brahman, the One without a second, the Bliss Absolute.

Samsara is the cycle of birth and death that exists until the realization of identity with Consciousness is established.

224. Once having realised Brahman, one no longer returns to the realm of transmigration. Therefore one must fully realise one's identity with Brahman.

225. Brahman is Existence, Knowledge, Infinity, pure, supreme, self-existent, eternal and indivisible Bliss, not different (in reality) from the individual soul, and devoid of interior or exterior. It is (ever) triumphant.

226. It is this Supreme Oneness which alone is real, since there is nothing else but the Self. Verily, there remains no other independent entity in the state of realisation of the highest Truth.

227. All this universe which through ignorance appears as of diverse forms, is nothing
else but Brahman which is absolutely free
from all the limitations of human thought.

228. A jar, though a modification of clay, is
not different from it; everywhere the jar is
essentially the same as the clay. Why then call
it a jar? It is fictitious, a fancied name merely.

229. None can demonstrate that the essence
of a jar is something other than the clay (of
which it is made). Hence the jar is merely
imagined (as separate) through delusion,
and the component clay alone is the abiding
reality in respect of it.

230. Similarly, the whole universe, being
the effect of the real Brahman, is in reality
nothing but Brahman. Its essence is That, and
it does not exist apart from It. He who says it
does is still under delusion - he babbles like
one asleep.

231. This universe is verily Brahman - such
is the august pronouncement of the Atharva
Veda. Therefore this universe is nothing but
Brahman, for that which is superimposed (on
something) has no separate existence from its
substratum.

*Atharva Veda is one of the four Vedas which
are also; Samaveda, Rigveda and Yayurveda.
The relative existence which is believed to have
an independent existence is none other than
Brahman.*

232. If the universe, as it is, be real, there
would be no cessation of the dualistic ele-
ment, the scriptures would be falsified, and
the Lord Himself would be guilty of an untr-
uth. None of these three is considered either
desirable or wholesome by the noble-minded.

233. The Lord, who knows the secret of all
things has supported this view in the words:
"But I am not in them" ... "nor are the beings
in Me".

4. This entire world is pervaded by Me in My Unmanifested form (aspect); all beings are in Me, but I do not dwell in them.

5. Nor do beings exist (in reality) in Me - see My Divine YOGA supporting all beings, but not residing in them, I am My Self, the competent cause of all beings.

234. If the universe be true, let it then be perceived in the state of deep sleep also.

As it is not at all perceived, it must be unreal and false, like dreams.

235. Therefore the universe does not exist apart from the Supreme Self; and the perception of its separateness is false like the qualities (of blueness etc., in the sky). Has a superimposed attribute any meaning apart from its substratum? It is the substratum which appears like that through delusion.

By ignorance, relative separate aspects are imposed on the absolute Consciousness which is already total, unified and irreconcilable.

236. Whatever a deluded man perceives through mistake, is Brahman and Brahman alone: The silver is nothing but the mother-of-pearl. It is Brahman which is always considered as this universe, whereas that which is superimposed on the Brahman, viz. the universe, is merely a name.

237-238. Hence whatever is manifested, viz. this universe, is the Supreme Brahman Itself, the Real, the One without a second, pure, the Essence of Knowledge, taintless, serene, devoid of beginning and end, beyond activity, the Essence of Bliss Absolute - transcending all the diversities created by Maya or Nescience, eternal, ever beyond the reach of pain, indivisible, immeasurable, formless, undifferentiated, nameless, immutable, self-luminous.

*Brahman, God-consciousness, is the only real,
the relative is an illusion which ignorance
regards as real.*

239. Sages realise the Supreme Truth, Brahman, in which there is no differentiation of knower, knowledge and known, which is infinite, transcendent, and the Essence of Knowledge Absolute.

240. Which can be neither thrown away nor taken up, which is beyond the reach of mind and speech, immeasurable, without beginning and end, the Whole, one's very Self, and of surpassing glory.

241-242. If thus the Shruti, in the dictum "Thou art That" (Tat-Tvam-Asi), repeatedly establishes the absolute identity of Brahman (or Ishwara) and Jiva, denoted by the terms That (Tat) and thou (Tvam) respectively, divesting these terms of their relative associations, then it is the identity of their implied, not literal, meanings which is sought to be inculcated; for they are of contradictory attributes to each other - like the sun and a glowworm, the king and a servant, the ocean and a well, or Mount Meru and an atom.

The problem with the statement 'You are That' (Tat-Tvam-Asi) is that as long as the identity with 'That' is the relative mind (Jīvan), this is not perceived as Brahman, but the identity is with the Jīvan.

243. This contradiction between them is created by superimposition, and is not something real. This superimposition, in the case of Ishwara (the Lord), is Maya or Nescience, which is the cause of Mahat and the rest, and in the case of the Jiva (the individual soul), listen - the five sheaths, which are the effects of Maya, stand for it.

If Ishwara (the Lord) is something imposed and dualistic as believed, this is Māyā or ignorance, as in the case of the Jiva (the individual soul).

244. These two are the superimpositions of Ishwara and the Jiva respectively, and when these are perfectly eliminated, there is neither Ishwara nor Jiva. A kingdom is the symbol of a king, and a shield of the soldier, and when these are taken away, there is neither king nor soldier.

245. The Vedas themselves in the words "now then is the injunction" etc., repudiate the duality imagined in Brahman. One must needs eliminate those two superimpositions by means of realisation supported by the authority of the Vedas.

The Vedas deny all duality attributed to Brahman. Peeling away all these claims is like peeling an onion that has a variety of layers, eventually emptiness is revealed, there is no material core.

246. Neither this gross nor this subtle universe (is the Atman). Being imagined, they are not real - like the snake seen in the rope, and

like dreams. Perfectly eliminating the objective world in this way by means of reasoning, one should next realise the oneness that underlies Ishwara and the Jiva.

The entity beyond Ishwara and Jivan is Brahman – ie. "Everything is Brahman". In the Absolute Now everything is real, even the illusion Māyā, which is then a real illusion. In relative existence, Māyā is always an illusion. As both Ishwara and Jivan are conceptual, they belong to the relative illusion.

247. Hence those two terms (Ishwara and Jiva) must be carefully considered through their implied meanings, so that their absolute identity may be established.

Neither the method of total rejection nor that of complete retention will do. One must reason out through the process which combines the two.

248-249. Just as in the sentence, "This is that

Devadatta", the identity is spoken of, eliminating the contradictory portions, so in the sentence "Thou art That", the wise man must give up the contradictory elements on both sides and recognise the identity of Ishwara and Jiva, noticing carefully the essence of both, which is Chit, Knowledge Absolute. Thus hundreds of scriptural texts inculcate the oneness and identity of Brahman and Jiva.

What determines the identity of Ishwara and Jīva is based on the level of awareness present ie. if they are considered from the mind or Consciousness.

250. Eliminating the not-Self, in the light of such passages as "It is not gross" etc., (one realises the Atman), which is self-established, unattached like the sky, and beyond the range of thought. Therefore dismiss this mere phantom of a body which thou perceivest and hast accepted as thy own self. By means of the purified understanding that thou art

Brahman, realise thy own self, the Knowledge Absolute.

It is important not to get caught up in the mind and intellect's way of describing Ātman and Brahman. As long as the awareness in Consciousness is not established, the mind and intellect can only proceed from ignorance and relative thinking.

251. All modifications of clay, such as the jar, which are always accepted by the mind as real, are (in reality) nothing but clay. Similarly, this entire universe which is produced from the real Brahman, is Brahman Itself and nothing but That. Because there is nothing else whatever but Brahman, and That is the only self-existent Reality, our very Self, therefore art thou that serene, pure, Supreme Brahman, the One without a second.

252. As the place, time, objects, knower, etc., called up in dream are all unreal, so is also the world experienced here in the waking sta-

te, for it is all an effect of one's own ignorance. Because this body, the organs, the Pranas, egoism, etc., are also thus unreal, therefore art thou that serene, pure, supreme Brahman, the One without a second.

253. (What is) erroneously supposed to exist in something, is, when the truth about it has been known, nothing but that substratum, and not at all different from it: The diversified dream universe (appears and) passes away in the dream itself.

Does it appear on waking as something distinct from one's own Self?

When the presence in Consciousness becomes reality, the unreal "dream universe" can no longer have an important role to play.

In sutras 254 – 263, Shankara gives various aspects of Brahman – Consciousness, to meditate upon.

254. That which is beyond caste and creed, family and lineage; devoid of name and form, merit and demerit; transcending space, time and sense-object - that Brahman art thou, meditate on this in thy mind.

255. That Supreme Brahman which is beyond the range of all speech, but accessible to the eye of pure illumination; which is pure, the Embodiment of Knowledge, the beginning-less entity - that Brahman art thou, meditate on this in thy mind.

256. That which is untouched by the sixfold wave; meditated upon by the Yogi's heart, but not grasped by the sense-organs; which the Buddhi cannot know; and which is unim-peachable - that Brahman art thou, meditate on this in thy mind.

"The Sixfold Wave"; Sri Shankara refers to six negative qualities such as; anger, decay, hung-er, thirst, sorrow and delusion.

257. That which is the substratum of the universe with its various subdivisions, which are all creations of delusion; which Itself has no other support; which is distinct from the gross and subtle; which has no parts, and has verily no exemplar - that Brahman art thou, meditate on this in thy mind.

258. That which is free from birth, growth, development, waste, disease and death; which is indestructible; which is the cause of the projection, maintenance and dissolution of the universe - that Brahman art thou, meditate on this in thy mind.

259. That which is free from differentiation; whose essence is never non-existent; which is unmoved like the ocean without waves; the ever-free; of indivisible Form - that Brahman art thou, meditate on this in thy mind.

260. That which, though One only, is the cause of the many; which refutes all other causes, but is Itself without cause; distinct from Maya

and its effect, the universe; and independent - that Brahman art thou, meditate on this in thy mind.

261. That which is free from duality; which is infinite and indestructible; distinct from the universe and Maya, supreme, eternal; which is undying Bliss; taintless - that Brahman art thou, meditate on this in thy mind.

262. That Reality which (though One) appears variously owing to delusion, taking on names and forms, attributes and changes, Itself always unchanged, like gold in its modifications - that Brahman art thou, meditate on this in thy mind.

263. That beyond which there is nothing; which shines even above Maya, which again is superior to its effect, the universe; the inmost Self of all, free from differentiation; the Real Self, the Existence-Knowledge-Bliss Absolute; infinite and immutable - that Brahman art thou, meditate on this in thy mind.

264. On the Truth, inculcated above, one must oneself meditate in one's mind, through the intellect, by means of the recognised arguments. By that means one will realise the truth free from doubt etc., like water in the palm of one's hand.

It is not possible to realize the truth only through faith and intellectual analysis, one must with the help of meditation experience the truth which is free from doubt as surely clair as the of seeing water in the palm of one's hand.

265. Realising in this body the Knowledge Absolute free from Nescience and its effects - like the king in an army - and being ever established in thy own Self by resting on that Knowledge, merge the universe in Brahman.

266. In the cave of the Buddhi there is the Brahman, distinct from the gross and subtle, the Existence Absolute, Supreme, the One without a second. For one who lives in this

cave as Brahman, O beloved, there is no more entrance into the mother's womb.

He who is constantly established and present in Consciousness has no need to be reborn.

267. Even after the Truth has been realised, there remains that strong, beginningless, obstinate impression that one is the agent and experiencer, which is the cause of one's transmigration. It has to be carefully removed by living in a state of constant identification with the Supreme Self. Sages call that Liberation which is the attenuation of Vasanas (impressions) here and now.

By being aware in Consciousness, the attachment to the mind can be subdued so that identification with Consciousness becomes established and constantly dominates awareness.

268. The idea of "me and mine" in the body, organs, etc., which are the non-Self - this superimposition the wise man must put a stop

to, by identifying himself with the Atman.
By identifying with Ātman, all dualistic influences fall away automatically.

269. Realising thy own Inmost Self, the Witness of the Buddhi and its modifications, and constantly revolving the positive thought, "I am That", conquer this identification with the non-Self.

Since everything is Consciousness, I should also be identified with Consciousness.

270. Relinquishing the observance of social formalities, giving up all ideas of trimming up the body, and avoiding too mush engrossment with the Scriptures, do away with the superimposition that has come upon thyself.

Following old fashioned unnecessary social behavior, unnaturally devoting oneself to one's body and becoming too preoccupied with the Scriptures binds and affects mind.

271. Owing to the desire to run after society, the passion for too much study of the Scriptures and the desire to keep the body in good trim, people cannot attain to proper Realisation.

272. For one who seeks deliverance from the prison of this world (Samsara), those three desires have been designated by the wise as strong iron fetters to shackle one's feet. He who is free from them truly attains to Liberation.

273. The lovely odour of the Agaru (agalochum) which is hidden by a powerful stench due to its contact with water etc., manifests itself as soon as the foreign smell has been fully removed by rubbing.

Agaru is a tree that has a strong aromatic scent that is used as a perfume, for incense and also in Ayurvedic treatments.

274. Like the fragrance of the sandal-wood,

the perfume of the Supreme Self, which is covered with the dust of endless, violent impressions imbedded in the mind, when purified by the constant friction of Knowledge, is (again) clearly perceived.

275. The desire for Self-realisation is obscured by innumerable desires for things other than the Self. When they have been destroyed by the constant attachment to the Self, the Atman clearly manifests Itself of Its own accord.

When the desire for the presence of Ātman becomes greater than anything else, the presence of Ātman becomes clear and real.

276. As the mind becomes gradually established in the Inmost Self, it proportionately gives up the desires for external objects. And when all such desires have been eliminated, there takes place the unobstructed realisation of the Atman.

277. The Yogi's mind dies, being constantly fixed on his own Self. Thence follows the cessation of desires. Therefore do away with thy superimposition.

278. Tamas is destroyed by both Sattva and Rajas, Rajas by Sattva, and Sattva dies when purified. Therefore do way with thy superimposition through the help of Sattva.

A purely sattvic awareness is interested in presence in Consciousness and not in creating new mental attachments, samskaras.

279. Knowing for certain that the Prarabdha work will maintain this body, remain quiet and do away with thy superimposition carefully and with patience.

Prārabdha is the karma that has shaped the present mental and bodily situation.

280. "I am not the individual soul, but the Supreme Brahman" - eliminating thus all

that is not-Self, do away with thy superimposition, which has come through the momentum of (past) impressions.

281. Realising thyself as the Self of all by means of Scripture, reasoning and by thy own realisation, do away thy superimposition, even when a trace of it seems to appear.

282. The sage has no connection with action, since he has no idea of accepting or giving up. Therefore, through constant engrossment on the Brahman, do away with thy superimposition.

The wise person is not bound by taking a position on the impact of the action but can act instinctively in the present without being so dependent on the past and the future. Both the past and the future are not real to the sage but only the present.

283. Through the realisation of the identity of Brahman and the soul, resulting from

such great dicta as "Thou art That", do away
with thy superimposition, with a view to strengthening thy identification with Brahman.

*The mental attachments are both from the past
and towards the future.*

284. Until the identification with this body
is completely rooted out, do away with thy
superimposition with watchfulness and a
concentrated mind.

285. So long as even a dream-like perception
of the universe and souls persists, do away
with thy superimposition, O learned man,
without the least break.

286. Without giving the slightest chance to
oblivion on account of sleep, concern in se-
cular matters or the sense-objects, reflect on
the Self in thy mind.

287. Shunning from a safe distance the
body which has come from impurities of

the parents and itself consists of flesh and impurities - as one does an outcast - be thou Brahman and realise the consummation of thy life.

288. Merging the finite soul in the Supreme Self, like the space enclosed by a jar in the infinite space, by means of meditation on their identity, always keep quiet, O sage.

289. Becoming thyself the self-effulgent Brahman, the substratum of all phenomena - as that Reality give up both the macrocosm and the microcosm, like two filthy receptacles.

Consciousness is present in, and the basis of, all phenomena both in macrocosm and microcosm.

290. Transferring the identification now rooted in the body to the Atman, the Existence-Knowledge-Bliss Absolute, and discarding the subtle body, be thou ever alone, independent.

291. That in which there is this reflection of
the universe, as of a city in a mirror - that
Brahman art thou; knowing this thou wilt
attain the consummation of thy life.

*To achieve the fulfillment of one's life is to rea-
lize that Consciousness - Brahman is you, as a
real knowing, insight and union and not as a
mere intellectual understanding or experience.
The highest knowledge is; that everything is
Consciousness.*

292. That which is real and one's own primeval Essence, that Knowledge and Bliss
Absolute, the One without a second, which
is beyond form and activity - attaining That
one should cease to identify oneself with
one's false bodies, like an actor giving up his
assumed mask.

293. This objective universe is absolutely
unreal; neither is egoism a reality, for it is
observed to be momentary. How can the perception, "I know all", be true of egoism etc.,
which are momentary?

294. But the real 'I" is that which witnesses
the ego and the rest. It exists always, even in
the state of profound sleep. The Shruti itself
says, "It is birthless, eternal", etc. Therefore
the Paramatman is different from the gross
and subtle bodies.

*That which witnesses the ego, sleep and dream
is the unborn, eternal Consciousness.*

295. The knower of all changes in things subject to change should necessarily be eternal
and changeless. The unreality of the gross
and subtle bodies is again and again clearly
observed in imagination, dream and profound sleep.

It is only the unchanging, eternal that can
experience the temporary changing. It is only
through duality that an experience or experience can arise.

296. Therefore give up the identification with
this lump of flesh, the gross body, as well as

with the ego or the subtle body, which are both imagined by the Buddhi.

Realising thy own Self, which is Knowledge Absolute and not to be denied in the past, present or future, attain to Peace.

Searching for lasting peace by using body and mind as tools means failure. Only by realizing presence in Consciousness can lasting peace be established.

297. Cease to identify thyself with the family, lineage, name, form and the order of life, which pertain to the body that is like a rotten corpse (to a man of realisation).

Similarly, giving up ideas of agency and so forth, which are attributes of the subtle body, be the Essence of Bliss Absolute.

Absolute Bliss does not arise as long as identification is bound to body and mind, but is established in Consciousness.

298. Other obstacles are also observed to
exist for men, which lead to transmigration.
The root of them, for the above reasons, is the
first modification of Nescience called egoism.

*As long as one identifies with the mind, egoism
is there as a cornerstone.*

299. So long as one has any relation to this
wicked ego, there should not be the least talk
about Liberation, which is unique.

*As ego is the opposite pole to the liberation
process, it is pointless to argue as this only leads to conflict. A certain awareness must exist
in order for the arguments to be able to land
on good ground.*

300. Freed from the clutches of egoism, as the
moon from those of Rahu, man attains to his
real nature, and becomes pure, infinite, ever
blissful and self-luminous.

(Rāhu was the son of the demon Vipracitti.)

301. That which has been created by the
Buddhi extremely deluded by Nescience, and
which is perceived in this body as "I am such
and such" - when that egoism is totally destroyed, one attains an unobstructed identity
with Brahman.

Blaming and referring to "that's how I am"
is the ego's way of denying bad actions. This
happens when the mind decides.

302. The treasure of the Bliss of Brahman
is coiled round by the mighty and dreadful
serpent of egoism, and guarded for its own
use by means of its three fierce hoods consisting of the three Gunas. Only the wise man,
destroying it by severing its three hoods with
the great sword of realisation in accordance
with the teachings of the Shrutis, can enjoy
this treasure which confers bliss.

An awareness that is not colored by the influ-
ence of the three gunas can experience pure
Consciousness – Bliss.

303. As long as there is a trace of poisoning left in the body, how can one hope for recovery? Similar is the effect of egoism on the Yogi's Liberation.

304. Through the complete cessation of egoism, through the stoppage of the diverse mental waves due to it, and through the discrimination of the inner Reality, one realises that Reality as "I am This".

"I am This" or "This is You" is expressed in Sanskrit "Tat Twam Asi".

305. Give up immediately thy identification with egoism, the agent, which is by its nature a modification, is endued with a reflection of the Self, and diverts one from being established in the Self - identifying thyself with which thou hast come by this relative existence, full of the miseries of birth, decay and death, though thou art the Witness, the Essence of Knowledge and Bliss Absolute.

306. But for thy identification with that egoism there can never be any transmigration for thee who art immutable and eternally the same, the Knowledge Absolute, omnipresent, the Bliss Absolute, and of untarnished glory.

Being identified with Consciousness means that there is no need for egoism and rebirth. Those who have the knowledge do not need to go to school to learn the knowledge.

307. Therefore destroying this egoism, thy enemy - which appears like a thorn sticking in the throat of a man taking meal - with the great sword of realisation, enjoy directly and freely the bliss of thy own empire, the majesty of the Atman.

308. Checking the activities of egoism etc., and giving up all attachment through the realisation of the Supreme Reality, be free from all duality through the enjoyment of the Bliss of Self, and remain quiet in Brahman, for thou hast attained thy infinite nature.

309. Even though completely rooted out,
this terrible egoism, if revolved in the mind
even for a moment, returns to life and creates
hundreds of mischiefs, like a cloud ushered
in by the wind during the rainy season.

310. Overpowering this enemy, egoism, not
a moment's respite should be given to it by
thinking on the sense-objects. That is verily
the cause of its coming back to life, like water
to a citron tree that has almost dried up.

*Many of the problems that exist in relative
existence can be traced back to egoism, both on
the individual and the collective level.*

311. He alone who has identified himself
with the body is greedy after sense-pleasures. How can one, devoid of the body-idea,
be greedy (like him)? Hence the tendency to
think on the sense-objects is verily the cause
of the bondage of transmigration, giving rise
to an idea of distinction or duality.

Being observant of egoism can help, but being present in Consciousness and thus ceasing to identify with the ego is the most effective.

312. When the effects are developed, the seed also is observed to be such, and when the effects are destroyed, the seed also is seen to be destroyed. Therefore one must subdue the effects.

Cause and effect are connected. If the cause disappear, the effect also disappear.

The desire for sense pleasures disappears if the sense pleasures disappear, of the pleasures disappear if the desire for sense pleasures disappear.

313. Through the increase of desires selfish work increases, and when there is an increase of selfish work, there is an increase of desire also. And man's transmigration is never at an end.

314. For the sake of breaking the chain of transmigration, the Sannyasin should burn to ashes those two; for thinking of the sense-objects and doing selfish acts lead to an increase of desires.

315-316. Augmented by these two, desires produce one's transmigration. The way to destroy these three, however, lies in looking upon everything, under all circumstances, always, everywhere and in all respects, as Brahman and Brahman alone. Through the strengthening of the longing to be one with Brahman, those three are annihilated.

317. With the cessation of selfish action the brooding on the sense-objects is stopped, which is followed by the destruction of desires. The destruction of desires is Liberation, and this is considered a s Liberation-in-life.

318. When the desire for realising Brahman has a marked manifestation, the egoistic desires readily vanish, as the most intense

darkness effectively vanishes before the glow of the rising sun.

319. Darkness and the numerous evils that attend on it are not noticed when the sun rises. Similarly, on the realisation of the Bliss Absolute, there is neither bondage nor the least trace of misery.

Those who are present in the darkness do not notice the light and those who are present in the light escape the darkness.

320. Causing the external and internal universe, which are now perceived, to vanish, and meditating on the Reality, the Bliss Embodied, one should pass one's time watchfully, if there be any residue of Prarabdha work left.

Prārabdha is the karma that has shaped the present mental and bodily situation.

321. One should never be careless in one's

steadfastness to Brahman. Bhagavan Sanatkumara, who is Brahma's son, has called inadvertence to be death itself.

322. There is no greater danger for the Jnanin than carelessness about his own real nature. From this comes delusion, thence egoism, this is followed by bondage, and then comes misery.

A Jñāni is one who consciously seeks knowledge and wisdom.

323. Finding even a wise man hankering after the sense-objects, oblivion torments him through the evil propensities of the Buddhi, as a woman does her doting paramour.

324. As sedge, even if removed, does not stay away for a moment, but covers the water again, so Maya or Nescience also covers even a wise man, if he is averse to meditation on the Self.

325. If the mind ever so slightly strays from the Ideal and becomes outgoing, then it goes down and down, just as a play-ball inadvertently dropped on the staircase bounds down from one step to another.

As long as one is bound and present in the mind, one becomes more and more bound to the sense sensations and loses contact with Consciousness. One who has once been consciously present in Consciousness, but loses contact, however, has no difficulty in becoming present in Consciousness again.

326. The mind that is attached to the sense-objects reflects on their qualities; from mature reflection arises desire, and after desiring a man sets about having that thing.

327. Hence to the discriminating knower of Brahman there is no worse death than inadvertence with regard to concentration. But the man who is concentrated attains comple-

te success. (Therefore) carefully concentrate thy mind (on Brahman).

Being present is the key to success in the contact with Consciousness. Especially at the moment of death there is every reason to be consciously present in Consciousness.

328. Through inadvertence a man deviates from his real nature, and the man who has thus deviated falls. The fallen man comes to ruin, and is scarcely seen to rise again.

For those who seek constant presence in Consciousness are in a process where you sometimes temporarily lose contact with Consciousness, but then regain it again. Consciousness never disappears.

329. Therefore one should give up reflecting on the sense-objects, which is the root of all mischief. He who is completely aloof even while living, is alone aloof after the dissolution of the body. The Yajur-Veda declares that

there is fear for one who sees the least bit of distinction.

Whoever is present in Consciousness is automatically distanced from the mind and the objects of the mind. No intellectual process is then needed to distance oneself.

330. Whenever the wise man sees the least difference in the infinite Brahman, at once that which he sees as different through mistake, becomes a source of terror to him.

The one who has realized "Brahman asi", i.e. all is Brahman even the objects of sense and the mind, need no longer worry.

331. He who identifies himself with the objective universe which has been denied by hundreds of Shrutis, Smritis and reasonings, experiences misery after misery, like a thief, for he does something forbidden.

332. He who has devoted himself to medi-

tation on the Reality (Brahman) and is free
from Nescience, attains to the eternal glory of
the Atman. But he who dwells on the unreal
(the universe) is destroyed. That this is so
is evidenced in the case of one who is not a
thief and one who is a thief.

333. The Sannyasin should give up dwelling
on the unreal, which causes bondage, and
should always fix his thoughts on the Atman
as "I myself am This".

*For the steadfastness in Brahman through the
realisation of one's identity with It gives rise to
bliss and thoroughly removes the misery born
of nescience, which one experiences (in the
ignorant state).*

334. The dwelling on external objects will
only intensify its fruits, viz. furthering evil
propensities, which grow worse and worse.
Knowing this through discrimination, one
should avoid external objects and constantly
apply oneself to meditation on the Atman.

Using objects as necessary tools is not problematic as long as one does not identify with the objects.

335. When the external world is shut out, the mind is cheerful, and cheerfulness of the mind brings on the vision of the Paramatman. When It is perfectly realised, the chain of birth and death is broken. Hence the shutting out of the external world is the stepping-stone to Liberation.

As long as the desires for sensepleasures and material objects are not extinguished, automatically incarnation will occur to satisfy the desires.

336. Where is the man who being learned, able to discriminate the real from the unreal, believing the Vedas as authority, fixing his gaze on the Atman, the Supreme Reality, and being a seeker after Liberation, will, like a child, consciously have recourse to the unreal (the universe) which will cause his fall.

337. There is no Liberation for one who has attachment to the body etc., and the liberated man has no identification with the body etc. The sleeping man is not awake, nor is the waking man asleep, for these two states are contradictory in nature.

The one who is liberated does not have any identification with the body, the mind or the ego, they are only tools to be able to navigate the relative existence.

338. He is free who, knowing through his mind the Self in moving and unmoving objects and observing It as their substratum, gives up all superimpositions and remains as the Absolute and the infinite Self.

To be free is to be consciously aware in both relative and absolute existence.

339. To realise the whole universe as the Self is the means of getting rid of bondage. There is nothing higher than identifying the uni-

verse with the Self. One realises this state by excluding the objective world through steadfastness in the eternal Atman.

By identifying with Consciousness is also identification with the universe.

340. How is the exclusion of the objective world possible for one who lives identified with the body, whose mind is attached to the perception of external objects, and who performs various acts for that end ? This exclusion should be carefully practised by sages who have renounced all kinds of duties and actions and objects, who are passionately devoted to the eternal Atman, and who wish to possess an undying bliss.

341. To the Sannyasin who has gone through the act of hearing, the Shruti passage, "Calm, self-controlled." Etc., prescribes Samadhi for realising the identity of the universe with the Self.

Being present in Samadhi requires no activity.

342. Even wise men cannot suddenly destroy egoism after it has once become strong, barring those who are perfectly calm through the Nirvikalpa Samadhi.

Desires are verily the effect of innumerable births.

Being fully present in Consciousness has the effect that the ego and selfishness no longer dominate.

343. The projecting power, through the aid of the veiling power, connects a man with the siren of an egoistic idea, and distracts him through the attributes of that.

Being tied to egoistic ideas can distract presence in Consciousness.

344. It is extremely difficult to conquer the projecting power unless the veiling power

is perfectly rooted out. And that covering over the Atman naturally vanishes when the subject is perfectly distinguished from the objects, like milk from water.

But the victory is undoubtedly (complete and) free from obstacles when there is no oscillation of the mind due to the unreal sense-objects.

Being able to distinguish the real from the unreal is the path to success for presence in Consciousness.

345. Perfect discrimination brought on by direct realisation distinguishes the true nature of the subject from that of the object, and breaks the bond of delusion created by Maya; and there is no more transmigration for one who has been freed from this.

346. The knowledge of the identity of the Jiva and Brahman entirely consumes the impenetrable forest of Avidya or Nescience. For

one who has realised the state of Oneness, is
there any seed left for future transmigration?

*When there is insight into the relationship
between Jivan and Brahman, ignorance disappears. Realizing this, there is no need to be
reborn.*

347. The veil that hides Truth vanishes only
when the Reality is fully realised.

*(Thence follow) the destruction of false know-
ledge and the cessation of misery brought
about by its distracting influence.*

348. These three are observed in the case of
a rope when its real nature is fully known.
Therefore the wise man should know the
real nature of things for the breaking of his
bonds.

349-350. Like iron manifesting as sparks
through contact with fire, the Buddhi manifests itself as knower and known through the

inherence of Brahman. As these two (knower and known), the effects of the Buddhi, are observed to be unreal in the case of delusion, dream and fancy, similarly, the modifications of the Prakriti, from egoism down to the body and all sense-objects are also unreal. Their unreality is verily due to their being subject to change every moment. But the Atman never changes.

As reality exists only in the present, where no change takes place and Ātman which never changes, then is the only reality.

351. The Supreme Self is ever of the nature of eternal, indivisible knowledge, one without a second, the Witness of the Buddhi and the rest, distinct from the gross and subtle, the implied meaning of the term and idea "I", the embodiment of inward, eternal bliss.

The Supreme Self is Absolute and beyond the relative Buddhi (intellect) etc.

352. The wise man, discriminating thus the
real and the unreal, ascertaining the Truth
through his illuminative insight, and realising
his own Self which is Knowledge Absolute,
gets rid of the obstructions and directly attains Peace.

353. When the Atman, the One without a
second, is realised by means of the Nirvikalpa
Samadhi, then the heart's knot of ignorance is
totally destroyed.

*In Nirvikalpa Samadhi which is Absolute
presence in Consciousness, Ātman, there is no
trace of ignorance only Absolute Knowledge.*

354. Such imaginations as "thou", "I" or "this"
take place through the defects of the Buddhi.
But when the Paramatman, the Absolute,
the One without a second, manifests Itself in
Samadhi, all such imaginations are dissolved
for the aspirant, through the realisation of the
truth of Brahman.

355. The Sannyasin, calm, self-controlled, perfectly retiring from the sense-world, forbearing, and devoting himself to the practice of Samadhi, always reflects on his own self being the Self of the whole universe. Destroying completely by this means the imaginations which are due to the gloom of ignorance, he lives blissfully as Brahman, free from action and the oscillations of the mind.

356. Those alone are free from the bondage of transmigration who, attaining Samadhi, have merged the objective world, the sense-organs, the mind, nay, the very ego, in the Atman, the Knowledge Absolute - and none else, who but dabble in second-hand talks.

When relative and absolute existence have been united, there is no reason to be reborn. Second-hand talks are conversations that are not anchored in Absolute Knowledge.

357. Through the diversity of the supervening conditions (Upadhis), a man is apt to think of

himself as also full of diversity; but with the removal of these he is again his own Self, the immutable. Therefore the wise man should ever devote himself to the practice of Nirvikalpa Samadhi, for the dissolution of the Upadhis.

Acting in the relative existence gives constant influence. Either this influence can flow off one like "water off a goose" or it can be retained in awareness. Presence in Nirvikalpa Samadhi neutralizes this influence, (Upadhi). Dysfunctional Upadhis give rise to suffering.

358. The man who is attached to the Real becomes Real, through his one-pointed devotion. Just as the cockroach thinking intently on the Bhramara is transformed into a Bhramara.

Bhramara is a bumblebee.

359. Just as the cockroach, giving up the attachment to all other actions, thinks intently

on the Bhramara and becomes transformed into that worm, exactly in the same manner the Yogi, meditating on the truth of the Paramatman, attains to It through his one-pointed devotion to that.

360. The truth of the Paramatman is extremely subtle, and cannot be reached by the gross outgoing tendency of the mind. It is only accessible to noble souls with perfectly pure minds, by means of Samadhi brought on by an extraordinary fineness of the mental state.

361. As gold purified by thorough heating on the fire gives up its impurities and attains to its own lustre, so the mind, through meditation, gives up its impurities of Sattva, Rajas and Tamas, and attains to the reality of Brahman.

362. When the mind, thus purified by constant practice, is merged in Brahman, then Samadhi passes on from the Savikalpa to the Nirvikalpa stage, and leads directly to

the realisation of the Bliss of Brahman, the One without a second.

Savikalpa Samadhi means temporary presence in Consciousness while Nirvikalpa Samadhi means permanent merging and presence in Consciousness.

363. By this Samadhi are destroyed all desires which are like knots, all work is at an end, and inside and out there takes place everywhere and always the spontaneous manifestation of one's real nature.

When the presence is in Consciousness, all striving for this spiritual union has ceased.

364. Reflection should be considered a hundred times superior to hearing, and meditation a hundred thousand times superior even to reflection, but the Nirvikalpa Samadhi is infinite in its results.

Presence in Nirvikalpa Samadhi is infinite-

ly superior to presence in the mind, ego and intellect.

365. By the Nirvikalpa Samadhi the truth of Brahman is clearly and definitely realised, but not otherwise, for then the mind, being unstable by nature, is apt to be mixed up with other perceptions.

366. Hence with the mind calm and the senses controlled always drown the mind in the Supreme Self that is within, and through the realisation of thy identity with that Reality destroy the darkness created by Nescience, which is without beginning.

Shankara here gives some advice for success in Yoga.

367. The first steps to Yoga are control of speech, non-receiving of gifts, entertaining of no expectations, freedom from activity, and always living in a retired place.

368. Living in a retired place serves to control the sense-organs, control of the senses helps to control the mind, through control of the mind egoism is destroyed; and this again gives the Yogi an unbroken realisation of the Bliss of Brahman.

Therefore the man of reflection should always strive only to control the mind.

Control of the mind provides control over egoism which lays the foundation for presence in Consciousness.

369. Restrain speech in the Manas, and restrain Manas in the Buddhi; this again restrain in the witness of Buddhi, and merging that also in the Infinite Absolute Self, attain to supreme Peace.

If presence in the mind is limited, presence in the Absolute Self ie. Consciousness takes place, and the effect of it, becomes supreme peace.

370. The body, Pranas, organs, manas, Buddhi and the rest - with whichsoever of these supervening adjuncts the mind is associated, the Yogi is transformed, as it were, into that.

371. When this is stopped, the man of reflection is found to be easily detached from everything, and to get the experience of an abundance of everlasting Bliss.

372. It is the man of dispassion (Vairagya) who is fit for this internal as well as external renunciation; for the dispassionate man, out of the desire to be free, relinquishes both internal and external attachment.

Sensual desire binds presence to mind and body. To be freed from this strong attachment requires presence in Consciousness which contributes to so much bliss (peace) that this state overshadows desire. Sensual desire never gives lasting satisfaction but must be constantly replenished, while spiritual satisfaction through presence in Consciousness does not need to be replenished.

373. It is only the dispassionate man who,
being thoroughly grounded in Brahman,
can give up the external attachment to the
sense-objects and the internal attachment for
egoism etc.

374. Know, O wise man, dispassion and discrimination to be like the two wings of a bird
in the case of an aspirant. Unless both are
there, none can, with the help of either one,
reach the creeper of Liberation that grows, as
it were, on the top of an edifice.

375. The extremely dispassionate man alone
has Samadhi, and the man of Samadhi alone
gets steady realisation; the man who has
realised the Truth is alone free from bondage,
and the free soul only experiences eternal
Bliss.

376. For the man of self-control I do not
find any better instrument of happiness
than dispassion, and if that is coupled with a
highly pure realisation of the Self, it conduces

to the suzerainty of absolute Independence; and since this is the gateway to the damsel of everlasting liberation, therefore for thy welfare, be dispassionate both internally and externally, and always fix thy mind on the eternal Self.

377. Sever thy craving for the sense-objects, which are like poison, for it is the very image of death, and giving up thy pride of caste, family and order of life, fling actions to a distance. Give up thy identification with such unreal things as the body, and fix thy mind on the Atman. For thou art really the Witness, Brahman, unshackled by the mind, the One without a second, and Supreme.

378. Fixing the mind firmly on the Ideal, Brahman, and restraining the external organs in their respective centres; with the body held steady and taking no thought for its maintenance; attaining identity with Brahman and being one with It - always drink joyfully of the Bliss of Brahman in thy own Self, without

a break. What is the use of other things which are entirely hollow?

379. Giving up the thought of the non-Self which is evil and productive of misery, think of the Self, the Bliss Absolute, which conduces to Liberation.

380. Here shines eternally the Atman, the Self-effulgent Witness of everything, which has the Buddhi for Its seat. Making this Atman which is distinct from the unreal, the goal, meditate on It as thy own Self, excluding all other thought.

Excluding all thoughts is not something that one should try to do. It happens automatically as the Bliss of Ātman overshadows all mental activity.

381. Reflecting on this Atman continuously and without any foreign thought intervening, one must distinctly realise It to be one's real Self.

It starts with paying attention; that one reali-
zes that one is not the body and the mind, this
leads to an awakening; which means a realiza-
tion that one has a body and a mind but that
the real identity is present in Consciousness,
which means enlightenment; when this presen-
ce becomes permanent.

382. Strengthening one's identification with This, and giving up that with egoism and the rest, one must live without any concern for them, as if they were trifling things, like a cracked jar or the like.

383. Fixing the purified mind in the Self, the Witness, the Knowledge Absolute, and slowly making it still, one must then realise one's own infinite Self.

The purification process of the mind enables presence in Consciousness as resulting in still-ness.

384. One should behold the Atman, the

Indivisible and Infinite, free from all limiting adjuncts such as the body, organs, Pranas, Manas and egoism, which are creations of one's own ignorance - like the infinite sky.

385. The sky, divested of the hundreds of limiting adjuncts such as a jar, a pitcher, a receptacle for grains or a needle, is one, and not diverse; exactly in a similar way the pure Brahman, when divested of egoism etc., is verily One.

386. The limiting adjuncts from Brahma down to a clump of grass are all wholly unreal. Therefore one should realise one's own Infinite Self as the only principle.

Brahma who creates the unreal relative existence must be seen in relation to the infinite Self.

387. That in which something is imagined to exist through error, is, when rightly discriminated, that thing itself, and not distinct from

it. When the error is gone, the reality about the snake falsely perceived becomes the rope. Similarly the universe is in reality the Atman.

388. The Self is Brahma, the Self is Vishnu, the Self is Indra, the Self is Shiva; the Self is all this universe. Nothing exists except the Self.

Brahman asi "Everything is Brahman".

389. The Self is within, and the Self is without; the Self is before and the Self is behind; the Self is in the south, and the Self is in the north; the Self likewise is above as also below.

390. As the wave, the foam, the whirlpool, the bubble, etc., are all in essence but water, similarly the Chit (Knowledge Absolute) is all this, from the body up to egoism. Everything is verily the Chit, homogeneous and pure.

391. All this universe known through spe-

ech and mind is nothing but Brahman; there is nothing besides Brahman, which exists beyond the utmost range of the Prakriti. Are the pitcher, jug, jar, etc., known to be distinct from the clay of which they are composed ? It is the deluded man who talks of "thou" and "I", as an effect of the wine of Maya.

392. The Shruti, in the passage, "Where one sees nothing else", etc., declares by an accumulation of verbs the absence of duality, in order to remove the false superimpositions. The Shruti are the sacred scriptures of Hinduism that aim to lead man away from ignorance and duality, to the truth.

393. The Supreme Brahman is, like the sky, pure, absolute, infinite, motionless and changeless, devoid of interior or exterior, the One Existence, without a second, and is one's own Self. Is there any other object of knowledge?

394. What is the use of dilating on this subject? The Jiva is no other than Brahman; this

whole extended universe is Brahman Itself;
the Shruti inculcates the Brahman without
a second; and it is an indubitable fact that
people of enlightened minds who know their
identity with Brahman and have given up
their connection with the objective world,
live palpably unifold with Brahman as Eternal Knowledge and Bliss.

395. (First) destroy the hopes raised by
egoism in this filthy gross body, then do the
same forcibly with the air-like subtle body;
and realising Brahman, the embodiment of
eternal Bliss - whose glories the Scriptures
proclaim - as thy own Self, live as Brahman.

396. So long as man has any regard for this
corpse-like body, he is impure, and suffers
from his enemies as also from birth, death
and disease; but when he thinks of himself as
pure, as the essence of good and immovable,
he assuredly becomes free from them; the
Shrutis also say this.

397. By the elimination of all apparent existences superimposed on the soul, the supreme Brahman, Infinite, the One without a second and beyond action, remains as Itself.

398. When the mind-functions are merged in the Paramatman, the Brahman, the Absolute, none of this phenomenal world is seen, whence it is reduced to mere talk.

When one is present in Consciousness, this is real, and not just talk of an altered state of consciousness, as is the experience in the phenomenal world.

399. In the One Entity (Brahman) the conception of the universe is a mere phantom. Whence can there be any diversity in That which is changeless, formless and Absolute?

400. In the One Entity devoid of the concepts of seer, seeing and seen - which is changeless, formless and Absolute - whence can there be any diversity?

401. In the One Entity which is changeless, formless and Absolute, and which is perfectly all-pervading and motionless like the ocean after the dissolution of the universe, whence can there be any diversity?

402. Where the root of delusion is dissolved like darkness in light - in the supreme Reality, the One without a second, the Absolute - whence can there be any diversity?

403. How can the talk of diversity apply to the Supreme Reality which is one and homogeneous ? Who has ever observed diversity in the unmixed bliss of the state of profound sleep?

404. Even before the realisation of the highest Truth, the universe does not exist in the Absolute Brahman, the Essence of Existence. In none of the three states of time is the snake ever observed in the rope, nor a drop of water in the mirage.

405. The Shrutis themselves declare that this dualistic universe is but a delusion from the standpoint of Absolute Truth. This is also experienced in the state of dreamless sleep.

406. That which is superimposed upon something else is observed by the wise to be identical with the substratum, as in the case of the rope appearing as the snake. The apparent difference depends solely on error.

407. This apparent universe has its root in the mind, and never persists after the mind is annihilated. Therefore dissolve the mind by concentrating it on the Supreme Self, which is thy inmost Essence.

408. The wise man realises in his heart, through Samadhi, the Infinite Brahman, which is something of the nature of eternal Knowledge and absolute Bliss, which has no

exemplar, which transcends all limitations, is ever free and without activity, and which is like the limitless sky, indivisible and absolute.

By being consciously present in Consciousness ie. in Samadhi, one need not speculate about the nature of absolute Bliss. This eternal Wisdom is revealed and not learned by the intellect.

409. The wise man realises in his heart, through Samadhi, the Infinite Brahman, which is devoid of the ideas of cause and effect, which is the Reality beyond all imaginations, homogeneous, matchless, beyond the range of proofs, established by the pronouncements of the Vedas, and ever familiar to us as the sense of the
ego.

410. The wise man realises in his heart, through Samadhi, the Infinite Brahman, which is undecaying and immortal, the positive Entity which precludes all negations,

which resembles the placid ocean and is without a name, in which there are neither merits nor demerits, and which is eternal, pacified and One.

411. With the mind restrained in Samadhi, behold in thy self the Atman, of infinite glory, cut off thy bondage strengthened by the impressions of previous births, and carefully attain the consummation of thy birth as a human being.

412. Meditate on the Atman, which resides in thee, which is devoid of all limiting adjuncts, the Existence-Knowledge-Bliss Absolute, the One without a second, and thou shalt no more come under the round of births and deaths.

413. After the body has once been cast off to a distance like a corpse, the sage never more attaches himself to it, though it is visible as an appearance, like the shadow of a man, owing to the experience of the effects of past deeds.

414. Realising the Atman, the eternal, pure
Knowledge and Bliss, throw far away this
limitation of a body, which is inert and filthy
by nature. Then remember it no more, for
something that has been vomited excites but
disgust when called in memory.

415. Burning all this, with its very root, in
the fire of Brahman, the Eternal and Absolute
Self, the truly wise man thereafter remains
alone, as the Atman, the eternal, pure Knowledge and Bliss.

416. The knower of Truth does no more care
whether this body, spun out by the threads
of Prarabdha work, falls or remains - like the
garland on a cow - for his mind-functions are
at rest in the Brahman, the Essence of Bliss.
Prarabdha is the part of the past karma
which is responsible for the present body.

417. Realising the Atman, the Infinite Bliss,
as his very Self, with what object, or for
whom, should the knower of Truth cherish
the body?

418. The Yogi who has attained perfection and is liberated-in-life gets this as result - he enjoys eternal Bliss in his mind, internally as well as externally.

419. The result of dispassion is knowledge, that of Knowledge is withdrawal from sense-pleasures, which leads to the experience of the Bliss of the Self, whence follows Peace.

420. If there is an absence of the succeeding stages, the preceding ones are futile. (When the series is perfect) the cessation of the objective world, extreme satisfaction, and matchless bliss follow as a matter of course. Being aware in the present gives access to reality and unparalleled happiness.

421. Being unruffled by earthly troubles is the result in question of knowledge.

How can a man who did various loathsome deeds during the state of delusion, commit the same afterwards, possessed of discrimination ?

Being present in Consciousness and being able to distinguish gives knowledge that provides a good starting point when delusion and dysfunctional states intrude.

422. The result of knowledge should be the turning away from unreal things, while attachment to these is the result of ignorance. This is observed in the case of one who knows a mirage and things of that sort, and one who does not. Otherwise, what other tangible result do the knowers of Brahman obtain!

423. If the heart's knot of ignorance is totally destroyed, what natural cause can there be for inducing such a man to selfish action, for he is averse to sense-pleasures?

He who is free from ignorance is also free from the selfish actions of the ego, is no longer interested in banal sense pleasures.

424. When the sense-objects excite no more

desire, then is the culmination of dispassion. The extreme perfection of knowledge is the absence of any impulsion of the egoistic idea. And the limit of self-withdrawal is reached when the mind-functions that have been merged, appear no more.

At a certain level of consciousness egoistic ideas and the mind functions no longer become dominant and present. Then they cannot arouse desire in order to thereby manifest themselves.

425. Freed from all sense of reality of the external sense-objects on account of his

always remaining merged in Brahman; only seeming to enjoy such sense-objects as are offered by others, like one sleepy, or like a child; beholding this world as one seen in dreams, and having cognition of it at chance moments - rare indeed is such a man, the enjoyer of the fruits of endless merit, and he alone is blessed and esteemed on earth.

*Being present in Consciousness means seeing
the objects of the senses as temporary and illu-
sory. This creates a relationship that is observing them. This non-attachment to the objects
of the senses means a blessed karma.*

426. That Sannyasin has got a steady illumination who, having his soul wholly merged in
Brahman, enjoys eternal bliss, is changeless
and free from activity.

427. That kind of mental function which co-
gnises only the identity of the Self and Brahman, purified of all adjuncts, which is free
from duality, and which concerns itself only
with Pure Intelligence, is called illumination.
*He who has this perfectly steady is called a
man of steady illumination.*

428. He whose illumination is steady, who
has constant bliss, and who has almost for-
gotten the phenomenal universe, is accepted
as a man liberated in this very life.

429. He who, even having his mind merged in Brahman, is nevertheless quite alert, but free at the same time from the characteristics of the waking state, and whose realisation is free from desires, is accepted as a man liberated-in-life.

430. He whose cares about the phenomenal state have been appeased, who, though possessed of a body consisting of parts, is yet devoid of parts, and whose mind is free from anxiety, is accepted as a man liberated-in-life.

The one who has changed through a shift, which means that the dominance of the mind has been broken and the presence in Consciousness has taken place has attained liberation.

431. The absence of the ideas of "I" and "mine" even in this existing body which follows as a shadow, is a characteristic of one liberated-in-life.

432. Not dwelling on enjoyments of the past,

taking no thought for the future and looking with indifference upon the present, are characteristics of one liberated-in- life.

Being present in Consciousness means that relative concepts such as the past, present and future are overshadowed by the eternal real presence.

433. Looking everywhere with an eye of equality in this world, full of elements possessing merits and demerits, and distinct by nature from one another, is a characteristic of one liberated-in-life.

For the one who is liberated, egoistic and greedy values become uninteresting, regardless of their merits and demerits. It is freed from the dominance of the mind, sees beyond all interpretations and concepts without being bound by them.

Resistance and conflict have been replaced by unity with the flow of life.

434. When things pleasant or painful present themselves, to remain unruffled in mind in both cases, through the sameness of attitude, is a characteristic of one liberated-in-life.

For one who is liberated and present in Consciousness, the normal activities of body and mind are not overshadowing. Being unmoved in the present does not mean that one is unaware or unable to act. It is the opposite; one is conscious and at the same time effective in acting without allowing the limitations of the mind to dominate.

435. The absence of all ideas of interior or exterior in the case of a Sannyasin, owing to his mind being engrossed in tasting the bliss of Brahman, is a characteristic of one liberated-in-life.

436. He who lives unconcerned, devoid of all ideas of "I" and "mine" with regard to the body, organs, etc., as well as to his duties, is known as a man liberated-in-life.

437. He who has realised his Brahmanhood aided by the Scriptures, and is free from the bondage of transmigration, is known as a man liberated-in-life.

438. He who never has the idea of "I" with regard to the body, organs, etc., nor that of "it" in respect of things other than these, is accepted as one liberated-in-life.

439. He who through his illumination never differentiates the Jiva and Brahman, nor the universe and Brahman, is known as a man liberated-in-life.

440. He who feels just the same when his body is either worshipped by the good or tormented by the wicked, is known as a man liberated-in-life.

441. The Sannyasin in whom the sense-objects directed by others are engulfed like flowing rivers in the sea and produce no change, owing to his identity with the Existence Absolute, is indeed liberated.

When the flowing river reaches the sea, there is a mixing that creates no visible change in the sea. This is similar to the shift of conscious presence from the mind to Consciousness.

442. For one who has realised the Truth of Brahman, there is no more attachment to the sense-objects as before: If there is, that man has not realised his identity with Brahman, but is one whose senses are outgoing in their tendency.

443. If it be urged that he is still attached to the sense-objects through the momentum of his old desires, the reply is - no, for desires get weakened through the realisation of one's identity with Brahman.

444. The propensities of even a confirmed libertine are checked in the presence of his mother; just so, when Brahman, the Bliss Absolute, has been realised, the man of realisation has no longer any worldly tendency.

445. One who is constantly practising meditation is observed to have external perceptions. The Shrutis mention Prarabdha work in the case of such a man, and we can infer this from results actually seen.

A realized one continues to have perceptions of relative existence.

446. Prarabdha work is acknowledged to persist so long as there is the perception of happiness and the like. Every result is preceded by an action, and nowhere is it seen to accrue independently of action.

Every action must be preceded by an underlying cause, according to the law of karma.

447. Through the realisation of one's identity with Brahman, all the accumulated actions of a hundred crore of cycles come to nought, like the actions of dream-state on awakening.

The dream state is seen as an illusion when

*one is awake, in the same way that all ac-
cumulated actions from the past are experienced as unreal in the present.*

448. Can the good actions or dreadful sins
that a man fancies himself doing in the dream-state, lead him to heaven or hell after he
has awakened from sleep?

449. Realising the Atman, which is unattached and indifferent like the sky, the aspirant is never touched in the least by actions
yet to be done.

*Both the past and the future are unreal illu-
sions. When one is present in Ātman and thus
present in the present, one realizes this. You
then have no worries about the past or the
future.*

450. The sky is not affected by the smell of
liquor merely through its connection with
the jar; similarly, the Atman is not, through
Its connection with the limitations, affected
by the properties thereof.

451. The work which has fashioned this body
prior to the dawning of knowledge, is not
destroyed by that knowledge without yielding
its fruits, like the arrow shot at an object.

452. The arrow which is shot at an object
with the idea that it is a tiger, does not, when
that object is perceived to be a cow, check
itself, but pierces the object with full force.

*If the cause is already established, the effect
cannot always be stopped.*

453. Prarabdha work is certainly very strong
for the man of realisation, and is spent only
by the actual experience of its fruit; while the
actions previously accumulated and those yet
to come are destroyed by the fire of perfect
knowledge. But none of the three at all affects
those who, realising their identity with Brahman, are always living absorbed in that idea.

They are verily the Transcendent Brahman.

The relationship to karma is completely dependent on the state of consciousness one is in.

454. For the sage who lives in his own Self as Brahman, the One without a second, devoid of identification with the limiting adjuncts, the question of the existence of Prarabdha work is meaningless, like the question of a man who has awakened from sleep having any connection with the objects seen in the dream-state.

Karma (prārabdha) has no function to fulfill for the one who is present in Consciousness.

455. The man who has awakened from sleep never has any idea of ”I” or ”mine” with regard to his dream-body and the dream-objects that ministered to that body, but lives quite awake, as his own Self.

When you wake up, it is obvious that the

dream was an illusion and is not related to the reality of the present.

456. He has no desire to substantiate the unreal objects, nor is he seen to maintain that dream-world. If he still clings to those unreal objects, he is emphatically declared to be not yet free from sleep.

457. Similarly, he who is absorbed in Brahman lives identified with that eternal Reality and beholds nothing else. As one has a memory of the objects seen in a dream, so the man of realisation has a memory of the everyday actions such as eating.

Whoever is not present in the illusion is no longer bound by what the illusion presents.

458. The body has been fashioned by Karma, so one may imagine Prarabdha work with reference to it. But it is not reasonable to attribute the same to the Atman, for the Atman is never the outcome of work.

Ātman, i.e. Consciousness, is not created and has a constant existence in the present. Ātman is not dependent on cause and effect or a result of activity.

459. The Shrutis, whose words are infallible, declare the Atman to be "birthless, eternal and undecaying". So, the man who lives identified with That, how can Prarabdha work be attributed?

460. Prarabdha work can be maintained only so long as one lives identified with the body. But no one admits that the man of realisation ever identifies himself with the body. Hence Prarabdha work should be rejected in his case.

461. The attributing of Prarabdha work to the body even is certainly an error. How can something that is superimposed (on another) have any existence, and how can that which is unreal have a birth? And how can that which has not been born at all, die? So how can

Prarabdha work exist for something that is unreal?

462-463. "If the effects of ignorance are destroyed with their root by knowledge, then how does the body live?" - it is to convince those fools who entertain a doubt like this, that the Shrutis, from a relative standpoint, hypothesise Prarabdha work, but not for proving the reality of the body etc., of the man of realisation.

464. There is only Brahman, the One without a second, infinite, without beginning or end, transcendent and changeless; there is no duality whatsoever in It.

465. There is only Brahman, the One without a second, the Essence of Existence, Knowledge and Eternal Bliss, and devoid of activity; there is no duality whatsoever in It.

466. There is only Brahman, the One without a second, which is within all, homogeneous,

infinite, endless, and all-pervading; there is no duality whatsoever in It.

467. There is only Brahman, the One without a second, which is neither to be shunned nor taken up nor accepted, and which is without any support, there is no duality whatsoever in It.

"There is only Brahman" can be said from a philosophical standpoint that is not anchored in an insight, but it can also be said from an insight that arises in the present and becomes self-evident. The insight arises when awareness is anchored in Consciousness.

468. There is only Brahman, the One without a second, beyond attributes, without parts, subtle, absolute and taintless; there is no duality whatsoever in It.

469. There is only Brahman, the One without a second, whose real nature is incomprehensible, and which is beyond the range of mind

and speech; there is no duality whatsoever in
It.

*It is not possible to experience Brahman, as an
experience requires duality, ie. something that
is experienced and someone who experiences.
As everything is Brahman there is no duality
and no experience.*

470. There is only Brahman, the One without
a second, the Reality, the One without a
second, the Reality, effulgent, self-existent,
pure, intelligent, and unlike anything finite;
there is no duality whatsoever in It.

471. High-souled Sannyasins who have
got rid of all attachment and discarded all
sense-enjoyments, and who are serene and
perfectly restrained, realise this Supreme
Truth and at the end attain the Supreme Bliss
through their Self-realisation.

*Self-realization means being constantly consci-
ously present in Consciousness.*

Rejecting the desire for sense pleasures then becomes natural and without a lack of sense pleasures.

472. Thou, too, discriminate this Supreme Truth, the real nature of the Self, which is Bliss undiluted, and shaking off thy delusion created by thy own mind, be free and illumined, and attain the consummation of thy life.

473. Through the Samadhi in which the mind has been perfectly stilled, visualise the Truth of the Self with the eye of clear realisation. If the meaning of the (Scriptural) words heard from the Guru is perfectly and indubitably discerned, then it can lead to no more doubt.

When awareness is established in Consciousness there is nothing to doubt and therefore nothing doubtful, as the truth gives clear insight.

474. In the realisation of the Atman, the Existence-Knowledge-Bliss Absolute, through the

breaking of one's connection with the bondage of Avidya or ignorance, the Scriptures, reasoning and the words of the Guru are the proofs, while one's own experience earned by concentrating the mind is another proof. Awareness in Consciousness brings truth and bliss and freedom from ignorance.

475. Bondage, liberation, satisfaction, anxiety, recovery from illness, hunger and other such things are known only to the man concerned, and knowledge of these to others is a mere inference.

476. The Gurus as well as the Shrutis instruct the disciple, standing aloof; while the man of realisation crosses (Avidya) through Illumination alone, backed by the grace of God.

There are certain phases of spiritual education that can only be obtained through God's grace in the present. Enlightenment is one such phase.

477. Himself knowing his indivisible Self through his own realisation and thus becoming perfect, a man should stand face to face with the Atman, with his mind free from dualistic ideas.

One who is realized does not experience Ātman as in a dualistic relationship, but is Ātman.

478. The verdict of all discussions on the Vedanta is that the Jiva and the whole universe are nothing but Brahman, and that liberation means abiding in Brahman, the indivisible Entity. While the Shrutis themselves are authority (for the statement) that Brahman is One without a second.

479. Realising, at a blessed moment, the Supreme Truth through the above instructions of the Guru, the authority of the Scriptures and his own reasoning, with his senses quieted and the mind concentrated, (the disciple) became immovable in form and perfectly established in the Atman.

When the mind is stilled and awareness is present in Ātman, Samadhi arises.

480. Concentrating the mind for some time on the Supreme Brahman, he rose, and out of supreme bliss spoke as follows.

481. My mind has vanished, and all its activities have melted, by realising the identity of the Self and Brahman; I do not know either this or not-this; nor what or how much the boundless Bliss (of Samadhi) is!

Even though the experience of the mind disappearing through the presence of Brahman, one realizes that the identity of Brahman is limitless, ie. includes everything, even the mind.

482. The majesty of the ocean of Supreme Brahman, replete with the swell of the nectar-like Bliss of the Self, is verily impossible to express in speech, nor can it be conceived by the mind - in an infinitesimal fraction of which my mind melted like a

hailstone getting merged in the ocean, and is
now satisfied with that Essence of Bliss.

*When awareness is in Consciousness which
gives the highest happiness, one is satisfied.*

483. Where is the universe gone, by whom is
it removed, and where is it merged?

It was just now seen by me, and has it ceased
to exist? It is passing strange!

*The universe, which has relative existence, is
perceived differently depending on the observer's state of consciousness.*

484. In the ocean of Brahman filled with the
nectar of Absolute Bliss, what is to be shunned and what accepted, what is other (than
oneself) and what different?

*"Ocean of Brahman" can be understood as
the eternal absolute ocean that generates Bliss
but also generates relative dualistic waves on*

*the surface, dualistically or nondualistically
depending on the observer's state of awareness.*

485. I neither see nor hear nor know
anything in this. I simply exist as the Self, the
eternal Bliss, distinct from everything else.

*Being present in Consciousness means being
in Bliss and not being bound or identified with
the mind and senses.*

486. Repeated salutations to thee, O noble
Teacher, who art devoid of attachment, the
best among the good souls and the embodiment of the essence of Eternal Bliss, the One
without a second - who art infinite and ever
the boundless ocean of mercy.

487. Whose glance, like the shower of concentrated moonbeams, has removed my
exhaustion brought on by the afflictions of
the world, and in a moment admitted me to
the undecaying status of the Atman, the Bliss
of infinite majesty!

488. Blessed am I; I have attained the consummation of my life, and am free from the clutches of transmigration; I am the Essence of Eternal Bliss, I am infinite - all through thy mercy!

489. I am unattached, I am disembodied, I am free from the subtle body, and undecaying, I am serene, I am infinite, I am taintless and eternal.

490. I am not the doer, I am not the experiencer, I am changeless and beyond activity; I am the essence of Pure Knowledge; I am Absolute and identified with Eternal Good.

491. I am indeed different from the seer, listener, speaker, doer and experiencer; I am the essence of Knowledge, eternal, without any break, beyond activity, limitless, unattached and infinite.

492. I am neither, this nor that, but the Supreme, the illuminer of both; I am indeed

Brahman, the One without a second, pure, devoid of interior or exterior and infinite.

493. I am indeed Brahman, the One without a second, matchless, the Reality that has no beginning, beyond such imagination as thou or I, or this or that, the Essence of Eternal Bliss, the Truth.

494. I am Narayana, the slayer of Naraka; I am the destroyer of Tripura, the Supreme Being, the Ruler; I am knowledge Absolute, the Witness of everything; I have no other Ruler but myself, I am devoid of the ideas of "I' and "mine".

Nārāyana is another name of Vishnu. The demon Nāraka was killed by Vishnu and the demon Tripura was killed by Shiva. God consciousness is "I" and "mine" and therefore can never observe itself, as there is no duality.

495. I alone reside as knowledge in all beings, being their internal and external support. I myself am the experiencer and all that is ex-

perienced - whatever I looked upon as "this"
or the not-Self previously.

*Only God-consciousness experiences and are
aware.*

496. In me, the ocean of Infinite Bliss, the waves of the universe are created and destroyed by the playing of the wind of Maya.

497. Such ideas as gross (or subtle) are erroneously imagined in me by people through the manifestation of things superimposed - just as in the indivisible and absolute time, cycles, years, half-years, seasons, etc., are imagined.

Sometimes people can have perceptions that do not match reality as they are based on old accumulated prejudices and imaginations.

498. That which is superimposed by the grossly ignorant fools can never taint the substratum: The great rush of waters observed in a mirage never wets the desert tracts.

Prejudices and imaginings that the mind constructs and do not match reality are as unreal as a mirage with water.

499. I am beyond contamination like the sky; I am distinct from things illumined, like the sun; I am always motionless like the mountain; I am limitless like the ocean.

500. I have no connection with the body, as the sky with clouds; so how can the states of wakefulness, dream and profound sleep, which are attributes of the body, affect me?

501. It is the Upadhi (superimposed attribute) that comes, and it is that alone which goes; that, again, performs actions and experiences (their fruits), that alone decays and dies, whereas I ever remain firm like the Kula mountain.

Upādhi are the illusions that prevent the attainment of liberation.

Kula Mountain is mountain in the Himalayas which is surrounded by beautiful valleys, rivers and forests.

502. For me who am always the same and devoid of parts, there is neither engaging in work nor cessation from it. How can that which is One, concentrated, without break and infinite like the sky, ever strive?

To be able to strive for something requires a desire for it. If the desire is not there, there is also no striving for it.

503. How can there be merits and demerits for me, who am without organs, without mind, changeless, and formless - who am the realisation of Bliss Absolute?

The Shruti also mentions this in the passage "Not touched", etc.

The Shruti Shankara refers to is Brihadaranyaka Upanisad IV 22; "In this state a father *is no father, a mother no mother, worlds no worlds, gods no gods, Vedas no Vedas. In this state thieves are not thieves, the murderer of a noble Brahmin not a murderer, a Candala (a caste) not a Candala, a Pulkasa (a caste) not a Pulkasa, a monk not a monk, a hermit not a hermit. In this state one is unmoved by good work and unmoved by evil work, as one is beyond all sufferings that touch the heart (intellect)."*

504. If heat or cold, or good or evil, happens to touch the shadow of a man's body, it affects not in the least the man himself, who is distinct from the shadow.

505. The properties of things observed do not affect the Witness, which is distinct from the, changeless and indifferent - as the properties of a room (do not affect) the lamp (that illumines it).

506. As the sun is a mere witness of men's actions, as fire burns everything without dis-

tinction, and as the rope is related to a thing superimposed on it, so am I, the unchangeable Self, the Intelligence Absolute.

507. I neither do nor make others do any action; I neither enjoy nor make others enjoy; I neither see nor make others see; I am that Self-effulgent, Transcendent Atman.

To identify with Ātman means to transcend relative existence and not to identify with it.

508. When the supervening adjunct (Upadhi) is moving, the resulting movement of the reflection is ascribed by fools to the object reflected, such as the sun, which is free from activity - (and they think) "I am the doer", "I am the experiencer", "I am killed, oh, alas!"

509. Let this inert body drop down in water or on land. I am not touched by its properties, like the sky by the properties of the jar.

510. The passing states of the Buddhi, such as

agency, experience, cunning, drunkenness, dullness, bondage and freedom, are never in reality in the Self, the Supreme Brahman, the Absolute, the one without a second.

Being present either in the relative existence or in the absolute existence are two completely different states of awareness that give different perceptions of reality.

Having presence simultaneously in both the relative and the absolute implies a unity consciousness, i.e. presence in Consciousness.

511. Let there be changes in the Prakriti in ten, a hundred, or a thousand ways, what have I, the unattached Knowledge Absolute, got to do with them ? Never do the clouds touch the sky!

To be unattached to the changes in Prakriti means not to be in conflict with relative existence.

512. I am verily that Brahman, the One without a second, which is like the sky, subtle, without beginning or end, in which the whole universe from the Undifferentiated down to the gross body, appears merely as a shadow.

Being aware in the present means being free and unbound in reality.

513. I am verily that Brahman, the One without a second, which is the support of all, which illumines all things, which has infinite forms, is omnipresent, devoid of multiplicity, eternal, pure, unmoved and absolute.

514. I am verily that Brahman, the One without a second, which transcends the endless differentiations of Maya, which is the inmost essence of all, is beyond the range of consciousness, and which is Truth, Knowledge, Infinity and Bliss Absolute.

515. I am without activity, changeless,

without parts, formless, absolute, eternal, without any other support, the One without a second.

516. I am the Universal, I am the All, I am transcendent, the One without a second.

I am Absolute and Infinite Knowledge, I am Bliss and indivisible.

517. This splendour of the sovereignty of Self-effulgence I have received by virtue of the supreme majesty of thy grace. Salutations to thee, O glorious, noble-minded Teacher, salutations again and again!

518. O Master, thou hast out of sheer grace awakened me from sleep and completely saved me, who was wandering, in an interminable dream, in a forest of birth, decay and death created by illusion, being tormented day after day by countless afflictions, and sorely troubled by the tiger of egoism.

Conscious presence can exist on three different levels of awareness.

- Since presence is anchored in body and mind, one is united and identified with body and mind, but is in duality with the rest of relative existence.

- When the conscious presence is anchored and identified with the Self (Ātman) one experiences duality to body and mind and the relative changing existence.

-When the conscious presence is anchored and identified with Consciousness (Brahman), the duality is gone and one is in unity with the relative and absolute aspects of existence (God Consciousness).

519. Salutations to thee, O Prince of Teachers, thou unnamable Greatness, that art ever the same and dost manifest thyself as this universe - thee I salute.

520. Seeing the worthy disciple, who had attained the Bliss of the self, realised the Truth and was glad at heart, thus prostrating himself, that noble, ideal Teacher again addressed the following excellent words:

521. The universe is an unbroken series of perceptions of Brahman; hence it is in all respects nothing but Brahman. See this with the eye of illumination and a serene mind, under all circumstances. Is one who has eyes ever found to see all around anything else but forms? Similarly, what is there except Brahman to engage the intellect of a man of realisation?

522. What wise man would discard that enjoyment of Supreme Bliss and revel in things unsubstantial ? When the exceedingly charming moon is shining, who would wish to look at a painted moon?

Why indulge in petty sense pleasures when you can experience supreme happiness, bliss and peace?

523. From the perception of unreal things there is neither satisfaction nor a cessation of misery. Therefore, being satisfied with the realisation of the Bliss Absolute, the One without a second, live happily in a state of identity with that Reality.

524. Beholding the Self alone in all circumstances, thinking of the Self, the One without a second, and enjoying the Bliss of the Self, pass thy time, O noble soul!

525. Dualistic conceptions in the Atman, the Infinite Knowledge, the Absolute, are like imagining castles in the air. Therefore, always identifying thyself with the Bliss Absolute, the One without a second, and thereby attaining Supreme Peace, remain quiet.

526. To the sage who has realised Brahman, the mind, which is the cause of unreal fancies, becomes perfectly tranquil. This verily is his state of quietude, in which, identified with Brahman, he has constant enjoyment of the Bliss Absolute, the One without a second.

He who is constantly consciously present in Consciousness also has his identity with Consciousness. This applies regardless of whether the person has a physical body or has left it.

527. To the man who has realised his own nature, and drinks the undiluted Bliss of the Self, there is nothing more exhilarating than the quietude that comes of a state of desire-lessness.

528. The illumined sage, whose only pleasure is in the Self, ever lives at ease, whether going or staying, sitting or lying, or in any other condition.

He who is present in Consciousness is not bound by time and space or whether the body is still or in motion.

529. The noble soul who has perfectly realised the Truth, and whose mind- functions meet with no obstruction, no more depends upon conditions of place, time, posture, di-

rection, moral disciplines, objects of meditation and so forth. What regulative conditions can there be in knowing one's own Self?

The noble soul that has no sensuous filters obscuring pure Consciousness, is present in Truth and is not bound to time and space, free from moral disciplines and objects of meditation.

530. To know that this is a jar, what condition, forsooth, is necessary except that the means of knowledge be free from defect, which alone ensures a cognition of the object?

531. So this Atman, which is an eternal verity, manifests Itself as soon as the right means of knowledge is present, and does not depend upon either place or time or (internal) purity. When Consciousness manifests, the relative mental and material existence arises.

Life takes up residence in relative existence and is present via knowledge that is adapted to the circumstances but at the same time unbound to neither place, time, nor inner purity.

532. The awareness that I am Devadatta (the devotee) who is independent of circumstances; similar is the case with the realization of the knower of Brahman, that he is Brahman.

As Brahman is everything, it is immaterial whether one has intellectual knowledge of Brahman or not.

533. What indeed can manifest That whose lustre, like the sun, causes the whole universe - unsubstantial, unreal, insignificant - to appear at all?

Consciousness, which is the cause of the manifested, is eternal and has never arisen and will never pass away.

534. What, indeed, can illumine that Eternal Subject by which the Vedas and Puranas and other Scriptures, as well as all beings are endowed with a meaning?

*There is a meaning to everything in manifested
existence.*

535. Here is the Self-effulgent Atman, of infinite power, beyond the range of conditioned
knowledge, yet the common experience of
all - realising which alone this incomparable
knower of Brahman lives his glorious life,
freed from bondage.

536. Satisfied with undiluted, constant Bliss,
he is neither grieved nor elated by sense-objects, is neither attached nor averse to them,
but always disports with the Self and takes
pleasure therein.

*To be constantly present in Consciousness
means a constant satisfaction in pure Bliss
Consciousness and at the same time an unbound attitude towards the mind and the
material objects.*

537. A child plays with its toys forgetting
hunger and bodily pains; exactly so does

the man of realisation take pleasure in the Reality, without ideas of "I" or "mine", and is happy.

One who is realized is no longer bound to the ego and its greed.

538. Men of realisation have their food without anxiety or humiliation by begging, and their drink from the water of rivers; they live freely and independently, and sleep without fear in cremation grounds or forests; their clothing may be the quarters them-selves, which need no washing and drying, or any bark etc., the earth is their bed; they roam in the avenue of the Vedanta; while their pastime is in the Supreme Brahman.

Sri Shankara here describes the life of an Indian monk. A sannyasi who has renounced material life to unite with the spiritual.

539. The knower of the Atman, who wears no outward mark and is unattached to external

things, rests on this body without identification, and experiences all sorts of sense-objects as they come, through others' wish, like a child.

A young child who has not begun to use the ego takes in sense impressions without dependence on identification and evaluation. The one who has knowledge of Ātman lives in a spiritual science without identifying it with the norms of the ego.

540. Established in the ethereal plane of Absolute Knowledge, he wanders in the world, sometimes like a madman, sometimes like a child and at other times like a ghoul, having no other clothes on his person except the quarters, or sometimes wearing clothes, or perhaps skins at other times.

541. The sage, living alone, enjoys the sense-objects, being the very embodiment of desirelessness - always satisfied with his own Self, and himself present at the All.

He who is present in Consciousness enjoys the objects of the senses without egoistic attachments, as he is present in the All.

542. Sometimes a fool, sometimes a sage, sometimes possessed of regal splendour; sometimes wandering, sometimes behaving like a motionless python, sometimes wearing a benignant expression; sometimes honoured, sometimes insulted, sometimes unknown - thus lives the man of realisation, ever happy with Supreme Bliss.

The person who no longer identifies with the body and mind can appear in different guises, but at the same time is judged differently by the environment, depending on the environment's level of awareness.

543. Though without riches, yet ever content; though helpless, yet very powerful, though not enjoying the sense-objects, yet eternally satisfied; though without an exemplar, yet looking upon all with an eye of equality.

544. Though doing, yet inactive; though experiencing fruits of past actions, yet untouched by them; though possessed of a body, yet without identification with it; though limited, yet omnipresent is he.

545. Neither pleasure nor pain, nor good nor evil, ever touches this knower of Brahman, who always lives without the body-idea.

Anyone who does not identify with the body and mind has undergone a paradigm shift which means awareness in Consciousness. The experience then is that one has a body and a mind and at the same time is identified with Consciousness.

There is then no dualistic conflict in this state of awareness.

546. Pleasure or pain, or good or evil, affects only him who has connections with the gross body etc., and identifies himself with these.

How can good or evil, or their effects, touch the sage who has identified himself with the Reality and thereby shattered his bondage?

547. The sun which appears to be, but is not actually, swallowed by Rahu, is said to be swallowed, on account of delusion, by people, not knowing the real nature of the sun.

In Hindu astrology, Rahu represents materialism, fear, dissatisfaction, obsession and confusion.

548. Similarly, ignorant people look upon the perfect knower of Brahman, who is wholly rid of bondages of the body etc., as possessed of the body, seeing but an appearance of it.

549. In reality, however, he rests discarding the body, like the snake its slough; and the body is moved hither and thither by the force of the Prana, just as it listeth.

When the snake has shed its skin, it no longer

*identifies itself with the skin, just as one who
is present in Consciousness no longer identifies
with body and mind.*

550. As a piece of wood is borne by the current to a high or low ground, so is his body carried on by the momentum of past actions to the varied experience of their fruits, as these present themselves in due course.

The results of actions (samskaras) become latent until they manifest themselves in the present.

551. The man of realisation, bereft of the body-idea, moves amid sense- enjoyments like a man subject to transmigration, through desires engendered by the Prarabdha work. He himself, however, lives unmoved in the body, like a witness, free from mental oscillations, like the pivot of the potter's wheel.

Even the one who is unaffected by relative existence is reminded of the pleasures of the senses via karma.

552. He neither directs the sense-organs to their objects nor detaches them from these, but stays like an unconcerned spectator. And he has not the least regard for the fruits of actions, his mind being thoroughly inebriated with drinking the undiluted elixir of the Bliss of the Atman.

Enjoyment from the sense organs gives rise to a certain measure of satisfaction.

Unfortunately, this is only a temporary transitory state of consciousness. Bliss comes from pure Consciousness (Atman) and is not temporary and not based on activities and experiences, but on presence in pure Consciousness. Pure Consciousness is not dependent on states of mind; wakefulness, dream or sleep.

The three states of mind; wakefulness, sleep and dream are relative states that can produce experiences. The fourth state of consciousness; turiya or transcendental Consciousness, is an absolute state that generates no experience.

553. He who, giving up all considerations of
the fitness or otherwise of objects of meditation, lives as the Absolute Atman, is verily
Shiva Himself, and he is the best among the
knowers of Brahman.

554. Through the destruction of limitations,
the perfect knower of Brahman is merged in
the One Brahman without a second - which
he had been all along - becomes very free
even while living, and attains the goal of his
life.

555. As an actor, when he puts on the dress
of his role, or when he does not, is always a
man, so the perfect knower of Brahman is
always Brahman and nothing else.

In the relative existence one takes on different roles, but the one who is present in Consciousness does not lose himself in the roles, he witnesses the relative existence and the states of awareness; wakefulness, sleep and dream. Witnessing the relative states of awareness, sleep and dream does not require wakefulness but only presence in absolute Consciousness.

556. Let the body of the Sannyasin who has realised his identity with Brahman, wither and fall anywhere like the leaf of a tree, (it is of little consequence to him, for) it has already been burnt by the fire of knowledge.

When the paradigm shift has taken place, the identification with the body and the mind has been moved from the body and the mind to Consciousness.

557. The sage who always lives in the Reality - Brahman - as Infinite Bliss, the One without a second, does not depend upon the customary considerations of place, time, etc., for giving up this mass of skin, flesh and filth.

558. For the giving up of the body is not
Liberation, nor that of the staff and the
water-bowl; but Liberation consists in the
destruction of the heart's knot which is Nescience.

*It is not enough for the monk, who only owns
a walking stick, a bowl of water and body and
mind, to give these up. The cause of ignorance
must be given up, which is absence of identification with, and awareness of Consciousness.*

559. If a leaf falls in a small stream, or a river,
or a place consecrated by Shiva, or in a crossing of roads, of what good or evil effect is
that to the tree?

560. The destruction of the body, organs,
Pranas and Buddhi is like that of a leaf or
flower or fruit (to a tree). It does not affect
the Atman, the Reality, the Embodiment of
Bliss - which is one's true nature. That survi-
ves, like the tree.

561. The Shrutis, by setting forth the real
nature of the Atman in the words, ”The Embodiment of Knowledge” etc., which indicate
Its Reality, speak of the destruction of the
apparent limitations merely.

562. The Shruti passage, ”Verily is this Atman
immortal, my dear”, mentions the immortality of the Atman in the midst of things perishable and subject to modification.

563. Just as a stone, a tree, grass, paddy, husk,
etc., when burnt, are reduced to earth (ashes)
only, even so the whole objective universe
comprising the body, organs, Pranas, Manas
and so forth, are, when burnt by the fire of
realisation, reduced to the Supreme Self.

*After the cessation of the physical organism,
the supreme Consciousness always remains.*

564. As darkness, which is distinct (from
sunshine), vanishes in the sun's radiance,
so the whole objective universe dissolves in
Brahman.

565. As, when a jar is broken, the space enclosed by it becomes palpably the limitless space, so when the apparent limitations are destroyed, the knower of Brahman verily becomes Brahman Itself.

566. As milk poured into milk, oil into oil, and water into water, becomes united and one with it, so the sage who has realised the Atman becomes one in the Atman.

567. Realising thus the extreme isolation that comes of disembodiedness, and becoming eternally identified with the Absolute Reality, Brahman, the sage no longer suffers transmigration.

568. *For his bodies, consisting of Nescience etc.,* having been burnt by the realisation of the identity of the Jiva and Brahman, he becomes Brahman Itself; and how can Brahman ever have rebirth?

569. Bondage and Liberation, which are con-

jured up by Maya, do not really exist in the Atman, one's Reality, as the appearance and exit of the snake do not abide in the rope, which suffers no change.

570. Bondage and Liberation may be talked of when there is the presence or absence of a covering veil. But there can be no covering veil for Brahman, which is always uncovered for want of a second thing besides Itself. If there be, the non-duality of Brahman will be contradicted, and the Shrutis can never brook duality.

571. Bondage and Liberation are attributes of the Buddhi which ignorant people falsely superimpose on the Reality, as the covering of the eyes by a cloud is transferred to the sun. For this Immutable Brahman is Knowledge Absolute, the One without a second and unattached.

Buddhi which is the intellect, is bound by its limitations and has no knowledge of the whole and the Absolute.

572. The idea that bondage exists, and the idea that it does not, are, with reference to the Reality, both attributes of the Buddhi merely, and never belong to the Eternal Reality, Brahman.

Brahman does not speculate as Buddhi does.

573. Hence this bondage and Liberation are created by Maya, and are not in the Atman. How can there be any idea of limitation with regard to the Supreme Truth, which is without parts, without activity, calm, unimpeachable, taintless, and One without a second, as there can be none with regard to the infinite sky?

574. There is neither death nor birth, neither a bound nor a struggling soul, neither a seeker after Liberation nor a liberated one - this is the ultimate truth.

575. I have today repeatedly revealed to thee, as to one's own son, this excellent and pro-

found secret, which is the inmost purport of all Vedanta, the crest of the Vedas - considering thee an aspirant after Liberation, purged of the taints of this Dark Age, and of a mind free from desires.

The secret is to free oneself from the sense sensations that give rise to desire, which cast a shadow over the crown jewel of the Vedas – Vivekacudamani i.e. Consciousness.

576. Hearing these words of the Guru, the disciple out of reverence prostrated himself before him, and with his permission went his way, freed from bondage.

577. And the Guru, with his mind steeped in the ocean of Existence and Bliss Absolute, roamed, verily purifying the whole world - all differentiating ideas banished from his mind.

578. Thus by way of a dialogue between the Teacher and the disciple, has the nature of the Atman been ascertained for the easy comprehension of seekers after Liberation.

579. May those Sannyasins who are seekers after Liberation, who have purged themselves of all taints of the mind by the observance of the prescribed methods, who are averse to worldly pleasures, and who are of serene minds, and take a delight in the Shruti - appreciate this salutary teaching!

580. For those who are afflicted, in the way of the world, by the burning pain due to the (scorching) sunshine of threefold misery, and who through delusion wander about in a desert in search of water - for them here is the triumphant message of Shankara pointing out, within easy reach, the soothing ocean of nectar, Brahman, the One without a second - to lead them on to Liberation.

That which bestows liberation – Consciousness, is never far away, it is always aware in the present, no matter which path we walk and no matter the suffering and pain the world inflicts, It is you! Tat Twam Asi!

*Shankara's message aims to lead to this libera-
tion!*

OM SHANTI SHANTI SHANTI!